Sparkling
THROUGH ADVERSITY

TRAVELING THROUGH LIFE'S TOUGHEST JOURNEYS WITH STYLE, GRACE, & SHINE!

TALESHIA L. CHANDLER, PH.D.

FOREWORD BY DR. ANTHONY M. CHANDLER, SR.

For permissions, inquiries or requests to book author for events, please send correspondence to:

U.S. Mail: 2301 Cedar Street, Richmond, VA 23223
Email: tcdst17@aol.com
Website: csbcog.org

Cover photos: Wanda Lewis / Alpha Images Photography
Cover design: Tobias McCain
Makeup: M.A.C.

Print ISBN: 978-1-7331181-0-1
Kindle ISBN: 978-1-7331181-1-8

Scriptures marked KJV are taken from the KING JAMES VERSION (KJV): KING JAMES VERSION, public domain.

Dedication

This book is dedicated in memory of:

Dr. Charles E. Booth

My father, Mr. Carlton Leroy Wilson

Ms. Louise Jeffries

My godmother, Mrs. Sarah Carolina Holmes

and

My beautiful saintly grandmother,
Mother Lucy Cornelia Gross,
affectionately known as "Mother Sunshine."
She taught me how to sparkle.

CONTENTS

Thank You...

God, You are just so good to me! I have to admit that my journey feels tough as nails, but as You promised, You have been with me every moment. "Thank You" is inadequate to tell You just how grateful I am for Your stripes and for my favorite, Jehovah Rapha! I pray that my witness to everyone about Your abounding love and healing power screams "Thank You" every day to You, My Father!

Anthony, my husband, soulmate, and best friend, for your unwavering love, support, care, protection, provision and passion for making my life as amazing and wonderful as possible amidst all that we have endured. I love you forever and always.

Anthony II (Ant), Alysha (Pumpkin), and Andrew (Buddy), my children, my loves, and my three heartbeats. Thank you for your unconditional love and for making me the proudest and happiest Mom ever! I absolutely love being your mother. Always remember that I love you more than words can express!

Mom, for your undeniable love, encouragement, and prayers. Out of all of the women in the world, I'm glad that God chose you for me! I honor you and Dad.

Tabitha (my Tamphy), my sister, my friend, for being so sweet and making me laugh uncontrollably, and for being sweet as pie! I love you Tamphena!!! Thank Ya Jeesuuusssssz! Lee, my superstar brother, I love you, "Sean Sean!"

My Queen (Mother Boobie Dear), thank you for not only being my mother in-law/my other Mom, but for being one of my best and most trusted friends and confidants. Our laughs and conversations are sacred, and I love you (and Uncle Billy) soooo much!!!!

Ms. Pat, my mother/sister/friend, assistant, laughing partner, and "roaddawg." God knew just who and what we both needed, and I appreciate all that you do for me in ministry and in life!

To my entire family! I love you all!!! Keep shining!

To ALL of my friends, especially GA, Tamara, Tamura, Courtney, Lisa, the Posse, Theresa and Darrick, Lauran, Karol, Paula, Marlene, Raynetta, Sonja (MP), my first lady sisters, Michael and Celeste, and you!

To my glam friends, Martina (Unleashed Salon) and Linh, for making me sparkle from head to toe!

To Dr. Kym Lee King, my beautiful big sis/Soror, for being a role model and for making one of my dreams (having my own lipstick ~TLC Pink) come true!

To my church family... there's no place like CSBC!

To Mr. Jermaine E. Harris. I'm forever indebted to you for being the first person to give me a chance in school administration. What a blessing to love my career and to enjoy going to work even on the days when I feel horrible. Your many lessons and ongoing mentorship are invaluable and sincerely appreciated. Educators can sparkle too!

To my Amelia family!

A special thank you to my oncologist, Dr. Joseph Evers...thank you for helping me to sparkle with your knowledge and wisdom. Please don't ever retire!!!

To Dr. Irby (thank you for listening to me), Dr. Sanni, Dr. Randolph, Nurse Molly, Dr. Monohan, Dr. Dameron and Ali (for giving me a sparkling smile), Dr. Smith (the good doc who answers my questions so that I won't Google), and Ms. Priscilla (you are irreplaceable)!

To my sister, friend, and favorite singer on the planet, Lady Karen Clark Sheard! Your inner beauty and humility make you sparkle. Thank you for allowing me to spend time with you and for bringing the sunshine in my life!

Lastly, thank you to Oprah Winfrey (my play aunt) and Michelle Obama (my play big sister). You can't sparkle without dreaming big!

Thank you for reading my book! Keep sparkling!!!

FOREWORD

"Her children arise up and call her blessed; her husband also, and he praiseth her. Many daughters have done virtuously, but thou excellest them all."

Proverbs 31:28-29

Job's wife is unapologetically, in my opinion, the most misunderstood and falsely accused person in the entire Bible. Because of a "truth or dare" battle between God, her husband and the devil, she lost everything that mattered to her: her home, children, fortune, extravagant way of living and almost her marriage. Such an unfair card was not just dealt to her husband, but her entire family. Subsequently, the title of "fool" was her noted award-winning title.

I think we owe Job's wife an apology for how we have for centuries berated this wife, mother, sister, partner and person. Unless you've walked miles in her shoes, you have no idea concerning the pain, misery, bereavement, loneliness and anger she must have experienced. A myriad of trouble followed by one phone call (messenger) changed the trajectory of her entire life, followed by many chapters plagued with dark days, miserable moments and many hard conversations.

How are we supposed to handle the trials and tribulations that God promised are just a fact of life? To hear the words that "you or your loved one has cancer," that "your baby has died," "you're fired," "your church has burned down," or any shocking situation that literally changes EVERYTHING, is certainly a fear that haunts every person and family. Sickness, disease, addiction, jail time and cancer, to name a few, all become game changers marking the beginning of a journey that is the culprit of fears you've never experienced, expenses you've never expected and many worries that will not afford you rest. This pain changes and discontinues almost all things you once enjoyed. Inevitably, you're forced to begin a chapter that challenges your faith in God and trust of people and relationships, in addition to daily avoiding the queries of mortality.

My wife, Dr. Taleshia Chandler, is the BOSS because she has picked up each of the stones "the universe" (as she says) has blatantly thrown at her and is mastering the art of sparkling through adversity. To many, it appears that she always does this with ease, but this is a misconception. I've watched her cry, witnessed the struggle and shared many unexpected curveballs that she has boldly conquered and enthusiastically overcome without missing a beat. She has mastered the art of sparkling in her workplace, social gatherings, church and even at home. She validates the theory that "You don't have to look like what you're going through!"

When faced with such adversities, most people have not been able to use these hardships to their advantage. Instead, they quit, lose hope and sadly succumb – failing to remember that we truly are the masters of our fate. I'm convinced that my wife is *stubbornly* the strongest person I've ever met. Quitting, not surviving and death have never been topics of discussion for us. She once said, "I'm not battling this cancer. *God* is!"

In this book, not only does Taleshia share intimate and extremely transparent details of her journey, but she also offers tools that will help you win through any misfortune. Ultimately, she challenges readers to walk in authority, put on your fight face, sound off with the lyrics of your favorite song and give it all that you've got left... and more!

Dr. Anthony Michael Chandler, Sr.
Proud Husband

1

But he was wounded for our transgressions, he was bruised for our iniquities: the chastisement of our peace was upon him; and with his stripes we are healed. —Isaiah 53:5

MY CURRENT SITUATION: TOUCHING LIVES & TAKING NAMES

If I had to write the story of my life, I would have originally written one different from the one I've lived for the past few years. You see, my life has included growing up in a great family with lots of care and attention. It's included being raised to have a reverence and heart for God and a sense of empathy and concern for others. It's included being surrounded by the best friends a girl could ever hope to experience in a lifetime. It's included advancing to the highest levels of my career and even earning my doctoral degree, something I'm super proud of. It even includes marrying the love of my life, my wonderful husband of 22 years, and parenting our three amazing children. Best of all, it has included fun... so much fun! I've traveled the world, sailed the oceans, eaten the most delicious food, met the most incredible people, and made memories that are more wonderful than I could ever have hoped to experience in life.

All of these elements are things that I would have surely written into the script, if I'd had the privilege of writing my own life's story. What I would not have written into the script is an experience that I have dreaded since childhood: cancer. That is, *originally*. I never would have written cancer into my script originally. However, a funny – and even kind of weird – thing happened after I got cancer. This dreaded disease affected my life in so many ways for the better that I have developed a great appreciation for how it has drastically changed me, and I don't know that I would have experienced such change any other way. Now, I know that writing my own life's story is not something that I can do; this is just a hypothetical discussion. However, my point is that while I never would have assigned myself cancer if I was writing the script, God thought otherwise. In His divine wisdom, by His sovereign choice, He allowed me to experience something I'd always dreaded because He not only knew the significant impact it would have on me, but on others that I would affect along the way.

So that you won't think that living with cancer has defined me, allow me to give you the back story that has led to where I am today. It all began with me meeting the man of my dreams, my co-star and leading man, my husband, Anthony. I met the man who would become my husband in high school when I was only 14 years old. I first saw him when I entered the 9th grade. As soon as I gathered up enough courage to approach him, I wrote him a letter telling him that I'd heard wedding bells. He wasn't interested – at all! Did I mention that I had a really bad Jheri curl at the time? Although I thought that I was just too cute with my glistening curl, it was a deterrent for him. Then, over the summer after my 9th grade year, I got a relaxer for the very first time in my life. When he saw me at the beginning of my 10th grade year, my hair was straightened and nicely styled, I'd gotten braces, so my teeth were straighter, and I was dressed in my cutest outfits. He couldn't resist the transformed Taleshia, and just like that, he became my boyfriend. We dated throughout high school with hearts fluttering and stars in our eyes. Everything was beautiful, because we were a bright young couple, happily in love.

Upon graduating from high school, I ended up going to the University of Maryland, and my husband attended Virginia Union University. According to my well-scripted plan, we were going to go to college for four years, graduate, and then get married. However, as things tend to go in real life, my plan experienced some hiccups. We broke up several times, but we always got back together again. Our last break-up, which was a really bad one, was so difficult for me that I went to talk to a trusted friend about it. When I told her, she got down on her knees and prayed to God, saying: "God, if this is Your will, heal this relationship and make this happen. In the meantime, please help Taleshia to move on and shift her focus from this relationship to completing her studies." That was it. We all need friends like her, the ones who have the sense to pray you through the difficulties of life instead of sitting there commiserating with you.

I went back to school my senior year of college, focused on my studies. Lo and behold, while I was minding my own business and living my life, Anthony called me out of the blue. Yep, you guessed it, we started dating again. We both graduated in 1995, and of course, attended each other's graduation ceremonies. At the end of 1995, Anthony proposed to me. We married in November, 1996. At our wedding, the same friend who had prayed that God would heal our relationship, if it was His will, was my bridesmaid. It's worth mentioning that at the wedding, she sang a rendition of "Great Is Thy Faithfulness" that was so amazing that it went viral, racking up more than 10 million views on social media! I truly believe that so many people were blessed by it because they could feel her sincerity in singing that song.

It was always a part of our plan that after completing our bachelor's degrees, we would both also pursue master's degrees. The question was not whether we would stick to this plan; it was about who would go back to school first. Well, I got pregnant three months into the marriage with our son, so it went without saying that he would go back to school first. My husband went to school at Howard University and earned his Master of Divinity. Each week, he traveled back and forth from Baltimore, Maryland to Washington, D.C., which was hard, because not only were we newlyweds, but we had a baby on the way. Once he finished, because he desired to work as a full-time pastor, he started submitting his resume to various churches as a pastoral candidate. His desire was not a surprise to me; he'd received his call to preach while we were still dating, and I was there when he preached his initial sermon. In fact, I was with him throughout his entire journey of preaching.

Eventually, after a very challenging application process, my husband was selected to pastor a church in our hometown, Baltimore, Maryland. He would be earning $300 per week, which meant that he still had to work another job in addition to pastoring. Although it was a small church that only had about 50 members, it looked like a grand cathedral to us! In fact, when he received the call and accepted the position, I felt really scared; I didn't feel like I was ready to be a first lady. Yes, I had grown up around church and knew what the expectations of a first lady were, but I was not sure that I had what it took to fill such a role. As I look back in retrospect, though, I recognize that God had already equipped me for everything I was going to be.

After my husband started pastoring, he went back to school in 2000 for his Doctorate of Ministry, completing it in 2003. After that, in 2004, I went back to school to get my master's degree. I'm a realist; I recognize that in education, it's hard to move up the career ladder without an advanced degree. I completed my master's degree in educational psychology from Walden University in 2006. Then, I entered the doctoral program at Walden University in 2006 and began pursuing my Ph.D.

Meanwhile, armed with a Doctorate of Ministry, my husband was ready to advance in his career. This time, the church that was interested in him was out of state in Richmond, Virginia. It was an amazing opportunity. So, after discussing it, we both agreed that he should take the job. Again, this was a scary season for me, because I'd never lived outside of Baltimore. Added to this were other not-so-small challenges: I was still enrolled in my Ph.D. program, and by this time, we were now a young family of five with two sons and one daughter. All of the support I relied on to help with the kids was in Baltimore; my mother and babysitter were always only a call away. I also loved the schools that my children attended in Baltimore. I wasn't ready.

Despite my initial tentative reaction, in order for this to work, my husband and I did what we had to do: we adapted. He went to Richmond to serve as the pastor of the church, and the children and I commuted back from Richmond to Baltimore every weekend, about a 2 ½- hour drive or a 3 ½-hour train ride each way. On Friday afternoons, I would pack up the kids and we would make the journey to Richmond, and on Sunday evenings after church, we would kiss my husband goodbye for another week and head back home. As soon as we got home, I would do all I could to prepare for the upcoming week, like ironing all of the kids' clothes for the week, grocery shopping, etc. I was also showing our house to prospective buyers at the time, because the kids and I would soon relocate from Baltimore to Richmond to be with my husband in his new church.

People would say to me, "Wow, Taleshia. You're doing a lot!" My response was that although it was hard, it was worth it. I traveled back and forth because I wanted the new church to know that my husband did actually have a wife and children. It was important to me that they saw his family there to support him when he stood before them each Sunday morning. In the end, I'm thankful that all of that worked during that season of our lives. I believe that God honored me for sticking it out and not being selfish. I really wanted the best for my husband, maximizing his potential, achieving all that he set out to accomplish in his education, and doing the job that he loved.

In July, 2008, the kids and I moved to Richmond to join my husband. Although it took me a little longer, in 2015, I graduated with my doctorate. Not only was my husband living the life he'd always wanted, but now I had a Ph.D. and was working in education, about to shoot up the career ladder in the field that I loved. I was the mother to three children who brought a smile to my face every day and the wife of a husband who loved me more than words could express. I was thrilled about the new experiences that lay ahead of me. I couldn't wait to get out there to do some singing, do some speaking, and to minister to others in my role as the first lady of a new ministry. There was nothing but untold potential, exciting adventures, great happiness and favor on the horizon. Life was about to take off for me!

And then... cancer.

If you read my first book, *A Divine Detour*, you've already read about the story surrounding my cancer diagnosis. I'm sure you'll agree that it's quite a story to tell. If you haven't already read my first book, let me give you the short version of what happened.

I felt that something was wrong. As women, we listen to the signals that our bodies send to us and the intuition that our senses use to signal us without a word. I went to my doctor and told her that something was wrong. She sent me to get a mammogram, and the mammogram did not indicate that anything was wrong. Despite the mammogram results, I knew that something was wrong. I just *knew*. I went from doctor to doctor, trying to sound the alarm that something was going wrong in my body, but no one would listen. By the time I got a doctor to listen, he sent me to get an MRI, and the results confirmed what I already knew: something was *very wrong*. I was diagnosed with stage 4 breast cancer seven months after I earned my doctorate.

As you can imagine, being diagnosed with breast cancer changed the entire trajectory of the life I had planned for myself. I took off work for a whole year. Over the years that followed, I went through what seemed like non-stop chemotherapy sessions and shots. During this time, I developed a habit of bringing a journal along to my chemotherapy sessions. In this journal, I would write personal reflections about things that were on my mind, thoughts and feelings about life and death, about God, about family, about perspective... everything. You see, at first, I couldn't understand why God would let me go through something so terrible, especially when, in my mind, I was doing all of the 'right' things. I've never missed a mammogram. I'm not the healthiest eater, but I've never smoked, done drugs, or drank alcohol. I try to live by all of the moral, ethical and spiritual principles my family taught me. I go to church. I pay my tithes. I help people. I've *always* tried to do the right thing. I'm not a perfect person, by far. I just felt like other people who were doing so much worse than what I'd done in life would have been better candidates for cancer. Instead, I was the one held hostage to sickness and feeling horrible while they were walking around fine and healthy, enjoying life.

I'm not going to lie to you and tell you that I didn't question God in the beginning. Yes, me... the strong, faith-filled, pastor's wife. I questioned God. I asked Him some serious questions, like, "Why are You punishing me? Why would You let them catch the cancer so *late*? Why wait until it's spread to my bones and liver before allowing the doctors to discover it? Why are You doing this to me, the one who always tries so hard to do all of the right things, of all people? Why do You think I deserve this?" I can't tell you how long I walked around shaking my head and trying to figure this out. Six words, which were part-statement and part-prayer, filled my thoughts day and night: "God, I just don't get it."

It's important for you to know something about me and cancer. Cancer has always been the one thing – that one particular thing out of all things that could possibly happen to me in life – that I have been deathly afraid of experiencing. In fact, I would see other women go through having cancer and pray, "Please, God. Please don't let me ever go through that." Nevertheless, in His sovereignty, He allowed it to be so. It took some time for me to realize that He was just allowing my life to take a detour to do some new, unplanned and different things – some great things that I never would have done on my own without a cancer diagnosis.

As God would have it, even though I never dreamt of being an author, I was able to turn the personal reflections that I'd written in my journal during chemotherapy about something terrible into something inspirational – my first book, *A Divine Detour: From Doctorate to Diagnosis to Destiny*. With this book, which

I published in 2016, God has allowed me to travel around the country to inspire others through words and through song. By giving my life a divine detour, He has taught me that even when we face what we consider to be the worst thing in the world, we can still be productive, positively impact the lives of others, and experience great joy.

Since the time that *A Divine Detour* was published, I have traveled to numerous churches, women's conferences and leadership conferences to talk about my story, raise awareness about women's health issues, share my testimony, and inspire others through word and song. I've had the opportunity to travel to new places, meet fascinating, new people, hear some incredible stories, and make new friends, all while signing and selling thousands of books. Best of all, I've received countless testimonies from people who have read *A Divine Detour*, telling me about how much it blessed their lives, changed their perspectives, and helped them to keep going amidst the challenges that they experienced.

I wrote this book as a continuation of A Divine Detour for two reasons. First, I wanted to inform those familiar with my story about all of the great things God has done in and through my life throughout my journey. At the end of my last book, I was functioning a lot better than the doctors expected. Today, I am still full of faith, singing His praises, and claiming my healing from the Lord! Second, I wanted to inspire others who might be going through a devastating life challenge of any type, sharing the lessons that I've learned along the way. When embraced, it is my hope that these lessons will help others navigate their own situations with sparkle, shine and grace.

My ultimate intent in writing this book is simple: I want to help people navigate devastating life challenges by teaching them to have a gratitude-focused perspective that compels them to live and enjoy every single day that they are blessed to be alive! It is my prayer that through the words in this book, you will be encouraged to sparkle through your own adversity or learn how to empower others who are facing their own difficult challenges in life to sparkle through with style and grace. After reading this book, may your life, and the lives of those around you, sparkle like never before!

2

*Fear thou not; for I am with thee: be not dismayed; for I am
thy God: I will strengthen thee; yea, I will help thee; yea,
I will uphold thee with the right hand of my righteousness.*
– Isaiah 41:10

"IF YOU HADN'T TOLD ME YOU HAD CANCER, I'D NEVER HAVE KNOWN" (...AND OTHER COMMENTS THAT TELL ME I'M KILLING IT WITH MY SPARKLE!)

You might wonder what makes me so sure that people want to hear my story. Am I right? I mean, come on. Let's face it. A cancer story doesn't exactly make for the most entertaining reading, right? Well, my story is different. My story is not a cancer story. Cancer does not define me. It is not even a part of my identity or who I am. Cancer is something that I am going *through*, period... and yes, I say "going through," because I know that it is not the end of things; healing is on the other side. The experience of cancer does not define me any more than your having the flu defines your identity. Who I am is much greater than cancer. Who I am is not even battling cancer. Who I am *beats* cancer! I'm living with it and conquering it every day with God's help.

This brings me to why I know that people want to hear my story. I can't tell you how many times people have come to me and said, "You know what? If you hadn't told me that you had cancer, I never would have known!" Other people who know me personally shake their heads and marvel at the way that I live life with my condition. Sometimes, they just stare at me in wonder. Other times, they'll come to me and say, "I don't get it! Some of the things I've always wanted to do, you're making happen, and you have cancer!" I give them a kind smile and offer a gracious "Thank you." To me, their words serve as affirmation that I'm absolutely killin' it (as the young people say) with sparkle and shine as I navigate my way through this difficult season of my life.

There's a reason that people are moved to say things like this to me. The reason: I don't look like what I'm going through! People look at my stylish self-presentation, my lighthearted disposition, the glow that I give off, my big, bright smile, and the faith that I display, and they'd never guess that I was experiencing such a devastating life challenge. They see me sailing away on cruises, going on girls' trips with my best friends, rolling with laughter with my close circle of friends in the corner of a restaurant, participating in ministry, singing my heart out, and inspiring others, and the thought of me having cancer would never pop into their minds, unless I told them. Most of all, people see my signature: my sparkle! They see my sparkly, bejeweled clothes, my bright sparkly accessories, my sparkly makeup, and even my cool sparkly nail polish. Altogether, the last thing that people would guess about me, unless I told them myself, is that I was dealing with stage 4 cancer!

I am often asked the question, "Taleshia, what's your secret? How in the world do you maintain such spirit, style and grace when you're dealing with something like this?" I'm always quick to say, "A little bit of MAC and a whole lotta Jesus!" I might share a tip or two here and there, but the "how" that they desire for me to explain to them is much more than can be explained in a casual 5-minute conversation. This is exactly why I'm so sure that people are interested in my story. They want to know how to maintain a sense of style, presence, poise and gracefulness as they go through their own life challenges... and in this book, I want to show them how.

It's funny. There is a common misconception that when you're going through something devastating, you should look like it. Because so many people buy into this misconception, when they are going through something, they feel like they are supposed to look the part. Better yet, they feel entitled to look the part, like because things are going horribly wrong in their lives, they have a right to take their focus and attention off of the way they present themselves and navigate life and to turn their complete focus and attention to their devastating situation. Their mindset is, "Yeah, I look a mess, like I've been going through hell, but it's okay. I have an exemption because my life is actually a mess and I am actually going through hell." They also tend to think, "It's okay for me to withdraw from life and spend my days alone in the dark because I'm going through something difficult. I have a good excuse to be depressed and unproductive because of what I'm going through. Those are the rules."

I'm here to tell you something different. I'm here to tell you that you do not have to look like what you're going through. I'm here to tell you that just because you're going through something devastating does not mean that you should stop living and enjoying life and helping others. I'm here to tell you that you have an option to sparkle through adversity with style and grace rather than looking like you've been run through the wringer. I'm here to give you the permission you need to live the life you've always wanted to live despite the unplanned circumstances that God has allowed to happen in your life. When you choose to live like someone who is determined to appreciate and enjoy life rather than resent and withdraw from it, people will be drawn to your story, too!

I've asked God to make a lot of things happen in my life in the past. I asked Him to do these things for me, but I realize after the fact that I did not ask Him how to make them happen. Today, I can say with all honesty that most of the things I've always wanted to do, the places I've always wanted to go, and the people that I've always wanted to meet, God allowed to be possible by allowing me to live with cancer. People reach out to me, want to meet me, want me to come speak and sing at their conferences, and want to know the story behind my shine because of how they see me overcoming adversity in my life. The cancer is the context that God has used to manifest many of the answers to my prayers! To be honest, I have asked, "God, couldn't you have used something else other than cancer to make my dreams come true?" His response: silence. I guess the answer is "No!" It was His choice and His plan. To that, I respond back, "Okay, then. Not my will, but Thy will be done!"

I say all of this to say that when God allows devastating circumstances to come into your life, you have a choice. Option one is that you can accept that it is His will, because He has a higher and greater plan that you could not possibly understand (even if He explained it to you), and choose to focus on enjoying the life you do have and the good you can still do for others. It's about going through life with style and grace. Option two is that you can keep on questioning, keep on resenting, allow bitterness to grow in your heart, and protest His sovereignty by withdrawing from Him, your relationships, and life. It's a decision that is completely up to you, and the choice you make will determine the quality of life that you live from that day forward. This option is about going through life looking beat-up, acting broken and being filled with bitterness and resentment. It's about going through life but missing out on life because you're so preoccupied with why such a thing happened to you and protesting about how unfair it is.

One of my favorite passages in the Bible is where Moses says, *"I have set before you life and death,"* and then he says, *"choose life"!* (Deut. 30:19). In the same way, if you are going through a devastating situation, I am setting before you at this very moment the opportunity to sparkle and shine through your situation or to allow your devastation to become evident in the way you present yourself, your perspective and your productivity. I encourage you to choose to sparkle and shine! I guarantee that it's a much better way to live life than the alternative. Dare to go through your situation in such a way that people can't look at you and tell that there's a whirlwind happening behind the scenes!

I'll be completely honest with you: It took some time for me to get where I am today, both mentally and emotionally. You've heard my story. When I was first diagnosed with stage 4 breast cancer, I was mad and angry. I felt like the doctors had failed me by not listening when I *insisted* that something was wrong. They completely let me down. Because of their negligence, my condition was allowed to progress from bad to worse – like, *stage 4 worse* – putting my life on the line. Their negligence threatened to remove a wife from her husband and a mother from her children. I had to fight like crazy not to carry bitterness and resentment in my heart for them for not taking my pleas for help seriously. However, instead of choosing to wallow in and nurture my bitterness and resentment, I let them go. They were counterproductive to what I needed to sparkle through and survive: hope.

If you're going to learn how to sparkle through adversity in a way that makes people want to know your survival "secret," you'll never be able to do it without hope. It's a small, four-letter word, but it carries great weight in your ability to overcome anything that life throws at you – things that God allows. You can't give up on hope, no matter what. I was diagnosed with cancer in 2015, and at the time of writing this book, it is 2019. The only reason that I have been able to sparkle through my own situation is because I have never completely given up hope. The hope I feel on the inside is the very thing that I exhibit on the outside. In other words, my hope is the source of my sparkle. Hope in what? Hope that what I am going through is temporary and not terminal. Hope that God will take care of me, regardless of what is happening in my life. Hope that as I focus on the here-and-now of today, God will take care of my tomorrow so that I don't have to worry about it. Hope that in the end, everything is going to be okay.

Sure, I've had my own moments of crying and sadness. However, I didn't allow myself to park there. Instead, I got up every day, put on my shiny lipstick and sparkling accessories, and made sure I looked my best as I went out into the world and did my best. Whatever I put my hand to, people know that I, the lady with the sparkles, give my all, whether at work, at church, in the community, or at a sorority meeting or event. I do all I can to ensure I give 100% effort to everything I do, because it is an outward manifestation of the hope that lies within me! Because of this, I make every day the best day possible. You'll be surprised at how focusing on looking your best, doing your best and being your best helps to shape your mood. It takes the focus away from the crying, sadness, depression and difficulty, and it helps to give you a more positive outlook on your situation and on life. I can't explain to you how it happens; I just know that it does happen. It really works!

Know that I am carrying you in my heart and praying for you as you read through this book. I have asked God to allow each person who reads it to be able to pick up something valuable that will completely change the way that they deal with their own adversity... that they learn how to sparkle through their struggles and situations rather than just endure them with sadness, waiting for them to pass.

If this book influences you to set up a trip and travel again (or even begin!), set up some fun lunch and dinner dates with your favorite people again, go put on some bright new lipstick, pull your favorite clothes and shoes out of the closet and put them on, spritz on some of your best cologne or perfume, get out and enjoy the sunshine, pick your favorite hobbies and activities back up again, dance like there's nobody watching, find unlimited reasons to smile each day, and savor life like there's no tomorrow, mission accomplished! My prayers will have been answered. I will have made an impact on your life by helping you to sparkle through adversity, and in doing so, helped you to begin living life again like it was meant to be lived!

3

I had fainted, unless I had believed to see the goodness of the Lord in the land of the living. Wait on the Lord: be of good courage, and he shall strengthen thine heart: wait, I say, on the Lord. – Psalm 27:13-14

~~CANCER~~ ANYTHING THAT DRAMATICALLY TURNS YOUR LIFE UPSIDE DOWN IS THE *WORST!*

The crazy thing about writing a book as someone who has cancer is that when people hear that you have cancer, they assume that the book is about cancer and that it will only be relevant to other people who are dealing with cancer. That's where they get it wrong. I shared with you that part of my reason for writing this book is to share some of the lessons that I have learned on my journey through adversity.

One of the biggest lessons that I have learned on my journey is that cancer is not the only devastating, life-altering challenge that can turn a person's life upside down. Not that it's a contest. There's no such thing as a "My adversity is bigger and more devastating than yours" contest. Even if there was, there would be no clear winner. The truth is that whatever life-altering, devastating thing that happens to you personally would come in first place on your list, so the descriptor "devastating" is relative. People are more likely to describe something using such a term if they have experienced something devastating themselves.

For example, if you were to put 100 people in a room and ask them what the most devastating thing they have ever experienced in life is, cancer would likely only appear on the lists of those who have had to deal with it – whose own lives or the lives of loved ones had been devastated by it. However, others would have their own response to "most devastating event." Some might say divorce, which can absolutely shatter a person's world. Some might say rape, which can traumatize a person for life, affecting the way they live forever. Others might say things like having a heart attack, getting a terminal illness other than cancer, being diagnosed with a debilitating mental illness, being violently attacked in a hate crime, losing a spouse or child, becoming paralyzed, losing their sense of sight or hearing, having a limb amputated, filing for bankruptcy, or even being deceived by a trusted friend or loved one. Each of these life events can change a person's life in unimaginable ways forever.

My point here is that cancer is not the only thing that's the pits. It's not the only thing that doesn't ask for permission to devastate your life. It's not the only thing that can turn your life upside down, making you deal with its effects forever. Cancer is not the clear winner of the "Life Devastation" prize. Therefore, someone who lives with cancer can't say to someone else who is going through their own devastation, "Stop whining! You haven't experienced *anything* until you've had cancer!" The other person would beg to differ, and in light of what I've learned on my own journey, so would I. If their life has been dramatically altered and turned upside down by something other than cancer, they *have* experienced something as equally devastating as cancer. It might not seem devastating to you, but it was devastating to *them*.

When I arrived at this realization, I knew that the book I was writing would not be about cancer. Instead, it would be for anyone going through any type of adversity or life-devastating event, because certain keys to getting through a life adversity are universal and timeless; they apply to everyone and do not change. Thus, whether you are dealing with divorce, illness, hurt, pain or loss of any type, the lessons that I teach about how to sparkle through adversity with style and grace can really help you!

There are certain traits that people who are living with adversity and life-altering situations have in common. I mention these so that you can understand that we're all in this together. We might be dealing with adversities of different types, but at the end of the day, all of us really have the same thoughts, feelings and needs that must be met. Here are some of the most common characteristics the people experiencing such situations share and my direct advice in response to each of them.

They feel like God has failed them and let them down.

If believers go through something traumatic or devastating, it is easy for one of the first questions that pops into their mind to be, "Why me, God? Why this?" Much of the time, people who say they have a relationship with God try to do the right thing. They might go to church (some more than others), treat others like they desire to be treated, and generally try to operate out of a sense of the types of ethics and moral behaviors that would be pleasing to God. Then, when God allows them to go through adversity, they feel that they have lived up to their part of the deal, but God has not... that God let them do all of the right stuff for years, but He did not reciprocate by doing "right" by them. Therefore, they feel like God let them down.

If you are experiencing this feeling, I have one encouragement for you: Don't give up on God. Yes, God could have prevented your situation from happening, but in His divine wisdom, He did not see fit to do so. What you must accept about God is that sometimes, His way might not seem like the right way, but the reality is that His way is perfect; it is always working to accomplish His will in our lives, even when we can't see how it could possibly be doing so. His way might not feel good; it might hurt like heck. However, while you are experiencing a depth of pain that you can't even explain – a pain too deep for words – you must simply accept that His way is the right way 100% of the time. He's God, so He doesn't have accidents or make mistakes. Everything that He does and allows is intentional.

Despite how much it hurts, always remember that the God of love, who loves you more than your mother and father, your spouse, your children, your friends, and more than any other being in the universe is capable of loving you, knows what is best for you. He hasn't forgotten about you. If you are His child, He lives in your heart, so He is right there with you as you go through your situation every single day. Rather than asking Him all of the "Why?" questions, ask Him to show you what you should be learning and whose life you should be touching through the experience. I know from my own personal journey that this is not easy to do; remember, I asked *lots* of "Why?" questions in the beginning of my own journey before I realized that the "Why?" didn't matter. As the Creator of the universe, He wasn't about to explain Himself to me anyway! Have faith in God. Trust in Him and give it time.

They experience sadness as an everyday feeling.

People who are dealing with life-altering adversity tend to feel sad – a lot. In fact, in the beginning, they can be so flooded with intense sadness – even deep-seated grief – that they can hardly function. In the midst of people and places that have always brought them great happiness, they are sad. When they watch television shows that used to make them laugh out loud, they can barely muster up a smile. Nothing is funny anymore. Even when they know that they are definitely experiencing something funny or amusing, and they know that they should be chuckling, or at least smiling, their body no longer responds to it the same way.

Things that once brought great joy and happiness no longer have this effect on them, as their lighthearted responses are drowned out by sadness. It's not that they are *trying* to be sad or that they are determined to be gloomy or depressed. They *want* to be happy. They just don't know how to anymore, in light of what they are going through.

When people come to me and explain that they are feeling like this, I take them through a special exercise. I ask them to think about the funniest thing that has ever happened to them or that they've ever seen. I ask them to consider it for a few moments. Once they have the funny incident in mind, I ask them to tell me about it. Then, I laugh about it. We continue to talk about how funny it was, and then they begin to laugh about it. Before you know it, we're laughing together – full, hearty, belly laughs!

The reason that I like to take people through this exercise is because of one of the greatest lessons that I've learned along my journey: laughter is contagious! It's kind of like yawning. Most of the time, all it takes is for one person to let out a big ol' yawn, and only seconds later, everyone else who saw the person yawn begins to yawn themselves. This is because yawning is contagious; once it starts, it's hard to stop! Laughter works the same way. The more you laugh, the more you continue to laugh!

I've even done this with my friends. We just started laughing out loud with one another for no reason. We weren't laughing at a joke, a story, something we'd seen – nothing. We just started laughing. The more we laughed at nothing, the more the laugh grew organically, all on its own. Rather than being manufactured, the laughter became genuine, so much so that we couldn't stop! Someone looking at us from the outside would have thought that we had just shared the joke of the century, but the truth was that we'd just begun laughing because we needed a laugh.

When you're going through the type of adversity that seems to suck all of the happiness and beauty out of life, it's common to ask questions like, "Will anything ever be funny to me again?" or "Will I ever laugh again?" The answer is yes. However, one might come before the other. You might begin to laugh again before anything ever becomes funny again. Yes, seeing and experiencing funny things provokes laughter more easily, but these things are not necessary to have a good laugh. All you really need for a good laugh is to have someone who wants to see you happy sit by your side and simply start laughing with you – at nothing at all! In time, as things even out in your situation and you start adapting to the reality of your newly-altered life, you'll be able to see funny things and be prompted to laugh. However, why wait until then? You can manufacture your own laugh right now!

They have lost hope and only see darkness in the distance.

Having a sense of hope suggests that you believe that there is a chance that what you are going through will get better and that your situation will change for the better. Many times, people who are struggling through adversity do not hold such a belief; they lose hope. When they look into the future (as if they really have the ability to do such a thing with any accuracy!) instead of seeing things differently than they are today, they see things remaining the same. Instead of seeing brighter days ahead, all they can see in the distance is darkness – complete and utter despair.

If you are in a state where you're not able to see anything but darkness and despair on the horizon, I have good news for you: if you take your focus off of your own situation and allow yourself to look outside of your own small world, you'll see something different – something that will give you *hope*! The only way to change what you see is to change what you're looking at, and what you look at is your choice alone. Don't like what you see? You can shift your eyes to look in another direction. Don't like what you see over there? Look at something else! Keep shifting your focus so that rather than seeing only darkness and despair, you begin to see things that foster hope.

Keep searching for new sights until you can fix your eyes on something that fills your heart with hope. If you would dare to take your focus off of the darkness and look at the light, I guarantee that you'll feel a greater sense of hope. After all, when you see others shining and surviving the same circumstances that you are going through, how can you not have hope? How can you not begin to believe that what you are going through will get better and something good can come out of what you are going through?

When you are only focused solely on your own situation, it can be easy to forget that there is a whole world out there with bright, beautiful things happening in it every day. People are surviving what you are going through with style and flair every day. People are smiling through the same circumstances that you are going through every day. Not only are they smiling and surviving the same situations that you are going through, but they are transforming their negative situations into something that has a positive impact on other people's lives. They are writing books, creating nonprofit organizations that provide assistance, volunteering with people affected by their type of adversity, and inspiring others by sharing their story.

I'm not a fortune teller, but I can tell you that things will change. They will get better. All throughout your life, you've experienced situations that you thought would never get better, but they all did. Somehow, things changed, and you went on to experience happiness. Just like those things changed, this will change. True, you might have to move on with a new-normal version of your life, but you will be able to move on with it and be happy. Allow this to feed your inner sense of hope, because you'll need it. Why? Because hope is what you're going to need to keep yourself going every single day of this journey.

They're really scared.

People who are experiencing adversity – real, life-changing, traumatizing adversity – get scared. They might not admit it aloud because they don't want to cause alarm with those who love them, but they are *really* scared. They are so afraid that often, they can't even pinpoint what they're afraid of clearly. At most, they can give you a list of things that sit at the forefront of their worst nightmares. For example, if they are dealing with something that's threatening their life, it's likely that they fear death. Facing the potential of death as a reality that could occur in the near future as opposed to something that will happen at some unknown time in the distant future can be terrifying.

Even if you have a relationship with God and you feel sure that you are going straight to heaven when you pass away, the idea of death can be scary. It's not that you're scared of being in heaven with God; it's that you're scared of not being on earth. You're consumed with what will happen to those that you have to leave behind, because you feel that no one can love, care for, or have their back like you can. You're scared of not seeing your children grow up, graduate, get married, and have families of their own because you know the pain they will face without you there.

People who are not dealing with life-threatening situations might fear other things that are just as scary. They might not be facing a loss of life; they might be facing loss of the quality of life or loss of someone significant in their life. These things can be so deeply and intensely painful that they can shatter a person's world and make them wish that they were dead. You do know that a lot of life situations can devastate a person to the point that they feel suicidal thoughts, right? The mere thought of going through a divorce, death of a spouse, or anything that means having to live without a beloved spouse can paralyze a person with fear. The idea of filing for bankruptcy, losing your house, car, and all of your assets and starting over from scratch, whether because of poor financial choices, loss of a job, or getting a serious disease that means you miss work too much can be so petrifying that it can make a person want to check out of life.

All trauma is scary and can easily fill us with fear. Traumatic, devastating situations change lives. When people realize that the experience they are facing is about to change their life in some way, it is the not knowing that's the most scary. We know how to navigate the normal lives that we live every day. What we don't know is whether we have what it will take to navigate the new normal that our devastating experiences thrust us into without our permission. That's the fearful part – the unknown.

If you're facing an experience that has your heart filled with fear, I have two words for you: trust God. If death is what you fear because you're not sure about where you're going after you die, trust God to save you, and then passionately pursue a relationship with Him. If you fear death because of those whom you'll have to leave behind on earth, trust God to take care of them; He is faithful, and believe it or not, He can do a better job taking care of them than you can. If your fear has to do with loss of stability, a radically-changed life, or even your quality of life being turned upside down by some unexpected circumstance, trust God to get you through these unknowns and to teach you how to thrive in your new normal.

Here's the good news: God is omniscient; He knows all things. You might not know what's going to happen to you tomorrow or in the days to come, but He does. He's already walked your life out from start to finish, and He knows what you need. Best of all, He will give you what you need right when you need it. You'll notice that I always talk about God giving you what you *need*, not what you *want*. If you could have everything that you wanted from God, you probably wouldn't be in your current situation anyway. God gives us what we need when we need it, because He's a good Father. He takes care of us well.

Always remember that God has not given us the spirit of fear, but of love, power and a sound mind (2 Timothy 1:7). He does not desire for us to walk around filled with fear; His will is for us to walk around filled of faith, trusting Him. Fear and faith cannot occupy the same space at the same time; it's one or the other. Therefore, choose faith. Be determined to walk in the soundness of mind that God has given us. Only with a sound mind can you focus on the here and now of what is actually happening today instead of speculating about the "mights" and "maybes" that are not guaranteed to happen tomorrow. A sound mind will help you to live your best life today, and you might as well learn to enjoy today, because tomorrow is not promised.

I can tell you from personal experience that allowing your mind to be consumed with fear about something that you have no control over anyway is such a waste. When I was first diagnosed with cancer, I was so consumed by fear that I couldn't sleep. I had insomnia for nearly the entire first year after my diagnosis. I would go to bed at bedtime, but then I would just lay there all night long, not sleeping. All night, my mind would race with questions and worry and other unproductive mental exercises that changed absolutely nothing. Then, after losing a year's worth of sleep, I said, "You know what? I don't even know when I'm gonna die. I'm just wasting time and missing out on stuff with all of this worry. I've had enough of this! No more focusing on dying. I'm about to live whatever life I have left like there's no tomorrow!"

The reality is that no matter how many "right" things you do or how clean you live, you don't know when the day will come when you take your last breath on earth. I was diagnosed with stage 4 cancer in 2015, but I don't even know if I'm going to die of cancer. I could choke on something, get into an auto accident, or be in the wrong place at the wrong time during a random robbery and die of a gunshot. Who knows how I'm going to die! Yes, most people assume that when a person gets cancer, that's eventually going to be their cause of death, but that's simply speculation. We simply don't know. Since this is true, why waste time trying to guess?

God uses things to remind me of this all the time. I can't tell you how many funerals I've been to where I've had to sing on the program for people who were at one point doing just fine, praying for me and encouraging me in my own journey. Then, unexpectedly, their day came and shocked us all. I was the one with cancer, but their day came before mine. Go figure. It's the realization that we just don't know what day is going to be our last that has helped me not to fear. Why waste my unknown number of days trying to control what I can't control and worry about what's going to happen, which is also beyond my control? Instead, I just take one day at a time. I enjoy today and do my best to make the most out of it. What's going to happen tomorrow is going to happen whether I obsess and worry about it or not.

These are the reasons why, instead of allowing my days to be filled with fear, I fill my days with faith, gratitude, and the people and things that make my heart overflow with happiness. My life is not dull, dark, gloomy and dreadfully morbid. I deliberately make sure that my life is rich, shining, bright, vibrant and sparkling! I sparkle through my adversity because it's *my* choice to do so!

4

For I know the thoughts that I think toward you, saith the Lord, thoughts of peace, and not of evil, to give you an expected end. – Jeremiah 29:11

SPARKLING THROUGH ADVERSITY: THE MENTALITY & WHAT IT MEANS

When you think about the word "sparkle," what comes to mind? If you're like most people, the image that pops into your head is something shiny, flashy and glimmering. If you were to look up the word "sparkle" in the dictionary, you would see words and phrases that describe something that is glittering, shimmering, twinkling, and even glowing, all of which make it entertaining to look at, because it *draws attention* to itself. Really think about that: sparkly things draw attention to their vibrancy. They don't seek to shrink away and hide in a corner!

When I describe myself as "sparkling through adversity," I am referring to a certain mentality of winning in the midst of devastating circumstances. This mentality is one that is focused on living a bright, shiny, vibrant life filled with light, love and laughter – even in the midst of adversity. Contrast this with a mentality that is focused on figuring out "why," harboring bitterness and resentment, feeling sorry for oneself, and withdrawing from life in order to concentrate on the unfairness of it all. Two mentalities. Two choices of how to think and live in the midst of adversity. One leads to a happy, brilliant life that attracts the attention of others and causes them to say, "Wow! Even with all they're going through, they are really living well. Look at *that!*" The other leads to a sad, dull life that doesn't want to be seen; it just wants to hide from each day and fade away in peace.

The sparkling through adversity mentality consists of the following eight aspects:

* Aspect 1: You make yourself and your life highly visible, because you want others to gain inspiration from your situation.
* Aspect 2: You determine to live each and every day of your life looking your best, doing your best and being your best, even though your situation is the worst.
* Aspect 3: You're not ashamed about what's happening to you; you embrace it and make the best of it.
* Aspect 4: You dare to still fully enjoy life, despite your devastating circumstances.
* Aspect 5: You're bold enough to be a model for others on how to live well when trauma occurs.
* Aspect 6: You refuse to cower in a corner and hide yourself from the world because of your situation.
* Aspect 7: You live a life filled with faith, trust in God, and hope rather than a life of fear, worry and doom.
* Aspect 8: You won't allow adversity to define and dominate your life; you make sure you outshine it by being far brighter than it is!

If you accept my challenge to sparkle through your adversity, two things will happen: your life will change, and you will inspire the lives of others who hear your story.

The reason that your life will change when you adopt the mentality of sparkling through adversity is because this is a mentality that helps you to look, do, and be your best every single day. I'm sure you know that this is not how people go through adversity. Usually, when people are going through adversity, their mentality is, "Hey... leave me alone. I'm doing the best I can. Don't you see what I'm going through?" They allow themselves a certain leeway in not looking their best, doing their best and being their best. However, people with a sparkle through adversity mentality don't give themselves such leeway. They give 100% of what they can every single day to looking, doing and being their best. Some days, they might be able to give more, and other days, they might not be able to give as much. The point is that they give all that they are capable of giving each day that they are alive, making the most out of life.

When you operate out of a mentality in which you strive to look your best, do your best and be your best, an amazing thing happens: you start *feeling* your best! I'm not a biopsychologist, so I can't really explain the scientific process behind the way it works. All I know is that it *really* does work! Not only do I know this from personal experience, but I know from the testimonies of others that I have encouraged to begin using this mentality that it has worked for them, too. You can probably reflect back on your own life and remember some times in the past when you looked and felt a mess, but then you cleaned yourself up and put on some nice clothes, and all of a sudden, you felt *great*! If it worked for you then, it will work for you now. What you do on the outside most definitely affects how you feel on the inside.

I make a bold effort to sparkle through adversity every day of my life. Sometimes, when I'm not having one of my better days, I might start the day off dragging around, looking and feeling a mess. When I do, I have to remind myself to sparkle. I don't give myself a reminder to sparkle because anyone is in my house watching me. You see, I don't just sparkle for others; I sparkle for myself! When I pull myself together, get cleaned up, put on a nice outfit, get my makeup right, and start sparkling, the difference in how I feel is like night and day. I feel so much better!

It's at these times, when I can activate my own "sparkle" in order to change the way I feel, that I'm thankful to God that I don't have to depend on anyone else to do this for me. All of the power that I need to feel better is within me; I don't have to wait on my family, my doctors, or anyone else to do it for me. All I have to do is take charge of my own life and put in the effort to sparkle in order to overcome the "blues" and other negative feelings that my devastating situation tries to flood my life with each day. I might not be able to control my situation, but I can control me in the midst of my situation. If I want to look, do, be, and feel better, it's all up to me. I have the ability to make myself have a better day every day that I want to. That's *such* an empowering thought!

I mentioned that if you accept my challenge to sparkle through your adversity, the other thing that would happen (in addition to your own life changing) is that you would inspire the lives of others who hear your story. I can't tell you how many people have reached out to me because of my sparkle. No, they don't come to me and say, "Hey, I saw you sparkling with your cancer and everything..." Instead, they say things that let me know they recognized my sparkle. Things like, "Your story has inspired me more than you know," and "You are truly an amazing person, and you give hope to so many people!" Without realizing it, they are saying that my story caught their attention because it was so sparkly, they couldn't miss it!

In order to be impacted by something, you have to see it. In the same way, in order for someone to be impacted by your story, you and your story have to shine. There is no way that you and your story are going to shine if you go through your experience like everyone else – with sadness, questioning, worry and withdrawal from life. The only way that you will be able to impact people with your story – to inspire them – is if you live it in an unusual and inspirational way.

Think about it. There are literally hundreds of thousands of people in the U.S. who have cancer. What causes people to reach out to me and ask me to come tell my story? Why are they calling me and not one of the hundreds of thousands of others who are dealing with the same thing? I'll tell you why. It's because I sparkle through my adversity. It's because I shine to the point that people can't help but notice. It's because I refuse to blend in with the way that "everyone else does it" and choose to stand out in the crowd. Because I choose to sparkle and shine in the midst of cancer, I have had the privilege to travel to places near and far to tell my story, share my book, touch lives through song, and inspire countless numbers of people around the nation. Their lives have been changed because I dared to sparkle through my adversity.

Here's my question to you: How will you, in the midst of your own adversity, stand out in the crowd? How will you shine? Will you go through your devastating situation the way that "everyone else does it," or will you do things so differently that people can't help but take notice and ask you how you do it? Remember: the first aspect of the sparkling through adversity mentality is that you make yourself and your life highly visible, because you want others to gain inspiration from your situation. You've got to really put on the sparkle so that you give them something to see that will result in them gaining hope, encouragement and inspiration.

One of the ways that a lot of people saw me standing out in my sparkle was through social media. Each time I would go to chemotherapy, I would take a selfie and post it online. I didn't just do it for the likes or to waste time because I was bored. Instead, I did it for a particular purpose. First, I posted on social media because I wanted to keep people updated on my progress. I wanted them to see that I was victorious and winning, not sad, sullen and feeling defeated. Second, I did it because I just knew I was too cute! I was looking *good* when I went to chemo! I would show them pics of my makeup and my outfit so that they could see me sparkling and standing out in the crowd. I was sure that they weren't used to seeing somebody go through cancer looking as good and as strong – physically and mentally – as I did! Finally, I posted on social media to inspire my followers, and in the process, give God glory for being with me every step of the way, just as He'd promised. I didn't post the pictures alone; I always accompanied them with an inspirational quote, a scripture, or something that was meant to inspire. Every post had a motive.

Altogether, I began posting on social media so that they could see that there was another way to go through a tough, devastating life circumstance.

Everybody already knows that you can look your worst when you're dealing with cancer or some other adversity. In fact, it's expected. However, for people to see me looking my best, strong in my faith, and seeking to encourage and inspire others when I was the one that they thought should be receiving the encouragement and inspiration was a big change. It made people sit up and take notice. A close friend, who has Lupus and has been through a *lot* on her journey with it, said that my posts inspired her and changed her life. They helped her overcome sadness and depression of her journey by dressing herself up, putting on makeup, getting out of the house again, and choosing to focus on the things that made her happiest – her grandchildren – instead of her disease. There were so many stories. My posts made people leave comments saying that I was an example for them, that they were always inspired after they saw my posts, that they'd never seen anyone deal with the disease like me, and that seeing me constantly smiling through my situation was amazing. Most of all, people asked that question that has become so familiar throughout my journey: "How do you do it?"

On the following pages are some photos (before & after my diagnosis) and screenshots of some social media images and messages that I've posted to share some sparkle and to spread God's light.

BCS (Before Cancer Sparkle)

Taleshia Chandler

I loved braids…never thought that something that simple could be taken for granted.

This is one of my favorite pictures! I felt like I was on top of the world... sparkling with my cinched waist, weave and heels!

Sparkling with knowledge... my first pic
after defending my dissertation, eight
months before my diagnosis.

Ph.D.s can sparkle too... limitless possibilities!

One month before diagnosis... tough workout
with my favorite trainer, Coach Bob!

I was in so much pain in this picture,
but I never suspected cancer.
I was smiling to encourage myself!

The big chop! This is the first pic taken after
I started losing my hair to chemotherapy.
Sparkling in my natural hair!

First photo shoot 2 months after starting chemo. Nothing sparkles like good make-up, denim and pearls!

Sparkle. Fight. Repeat.

My favorite denim jacket... pop your collar
for added sparkle!

Surprise birthday party!

Is this party for me?

Smiles. Soulmates. Sparkling.

Denim (with popped collar) + blonde + smile =
Sparkling!

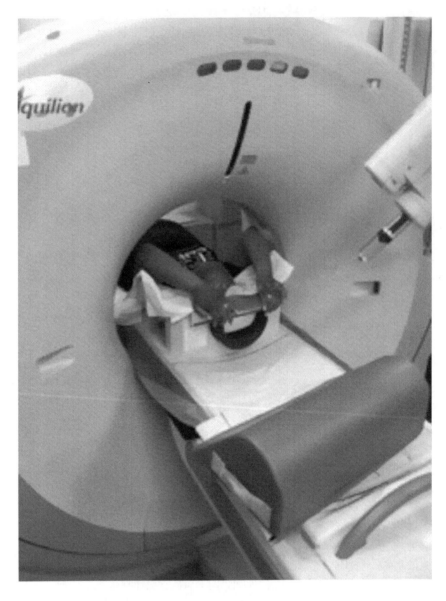

Sparkling through "Scanxiety"

Day after chemo sparkle!

Your sparkle should have depth and substance!

Mood after surrendering to His will

3 Year Conqueror

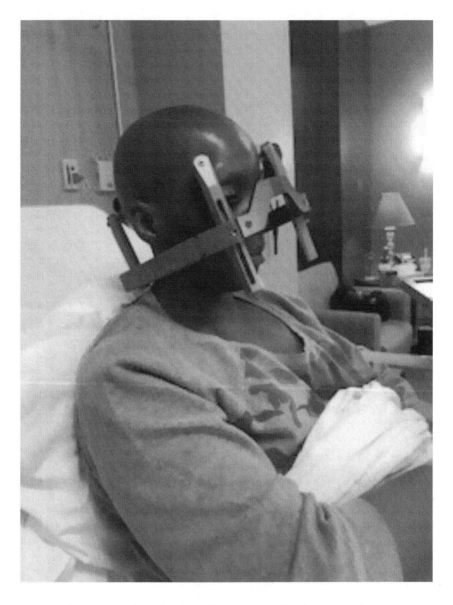

Gamma Knife Radiation ~ 5 days before
my 45th birthday.

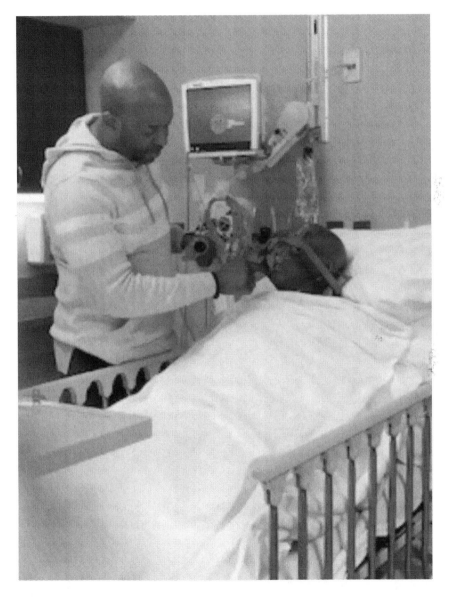

My favorite traveling companion helping me
to sparkle through adversity.

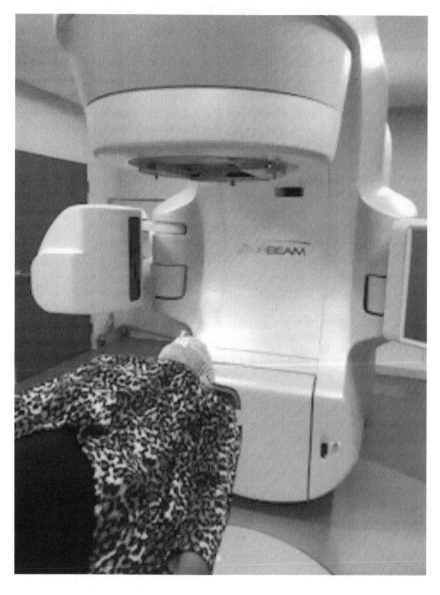

Radiation... leopard print. Why not!

3 days after Gamma Knife surgery/radiation:
sequined black pants + denim jacket (of course) =
Sparkl!ing!

Singing through adversity!

"I cried my last tear Yesterday!"

Going to my first treatment yesterday and this song came on the radio. I love you **Taleshia Chandler!!!**

 Taleshia Chandler is with **Tabitha Brooks.**
October 6, 2016 · 🌐

Hey! My sister sent me this clip of my first chemotherapy session. I gave God praise right in my car! Just wanted to share it and dedicate... Continue Reading

First chemotherapy session. Singing "Destiny."

Taleshia Chandler is with **Pat Morgan**.
November 16, 2018 · 🌐

Happy Friday! Living with cancer is really rough; but, I refuse
to let it ruin my exciting weekend and Thanksgiving!
#MichelleObamabooktour #ThanksgivinginBaltimore
#somanyreasonstosmile

👍❤️ 645   153 Comments   1 Share

Chemo. Favorite denim jacket. Glitter ribbon.

"Let's Make A Deal" Breast Cancer Warrior!

 **Taleshia Chandler**
December 14, 2018 · 🌐

Hey good people! My doc had to postpone chemo to handle a "life-threatening" issue. So, I called all of the prayer warriors and God did it again!!! Whatever you're facing today, just sparkle on through it with Jesus!!! #adivinedetour #chemoday #mymedicalteamisanointed #madeittoclub45intheprocess #thanksfortheprayers #JehovahRapha #myhusbandisamazing #mym... See More

559   130 Comments 1 Share

Steroids and a shiny star. Sparkling!

Taleshia Chandler
January 4 · 🌐

Chemo Day. Psalm 27:13-14 #adivinedetour #hello2019
#withmyBaybey🤍 Anthony Michael Chandler😌

👍❤️ 464   84 Comments 2 Shares

👍 Like   💬 Comment   ➤ Share

 Lisa King
Yes!!!! It's already done!!🙌🙌🙌😘

Taleshia Chandler
January 25 · 🌐

Although I was diagnosed with breast cancer in 2015, it is still hard to accept most days. I trust God and He has been consistently faithful. So, I feel guilty for feeling scared & so nervous about things like my scans (I have a ton of them next month😳) as if I don't know what God has already done nor what the Bible says about having a "spirit of fear." I heard a very liberating phrase in church from Bis... See More

‹ Taleshia's Post

12/4/18 ~ Brain surgery/ radiation to treat 4 malignant lesions (of which one the doctor stated treating it was a matter of life or death)

12/8/18 ~ celebrated 45th birthday!

12/10-14/18 ~ brain radiation every day

1/1/19 ~ father passed away

2/2/19 ~ follow-up MRI

2/7/19 ~ Doctor informs me that the 4 lesions have resolved and 2 lesions are completely undetectable! 😵😵😵 (Won't God do it!!!!!!)

Every day ~ me thanking God for doing it AGAIN!!!!!!! I probably would have written the script differently; but at this point, I choose to just trust God's plan! (Jer. 29:11)

Today ~ reviewing the first draft of my 2nd book at chemo!!!!

#adivinedetour #coveredbyangels #GrandmaLucy #book2comingsoon #Goddidit #ohyeahthatsbae😵 #blessed #THANKFUL

⭕💙😮 657   199 Comments 10 Shares

👍 Like   💬 Comment   ↪ Share

 **Taleshia Chandler**
March 8 · 🌐

Happy Friday to everyone and a special shout out to all of my amazing sisters everywhere...Happy International Women's Day! (hi @oprah, @michelleobama and @karenclarksheard 😊💜👑)!!!!
#adivinedetour
#thislittlelightofmineimgonnaletitSPARKLE🕯️💥✨

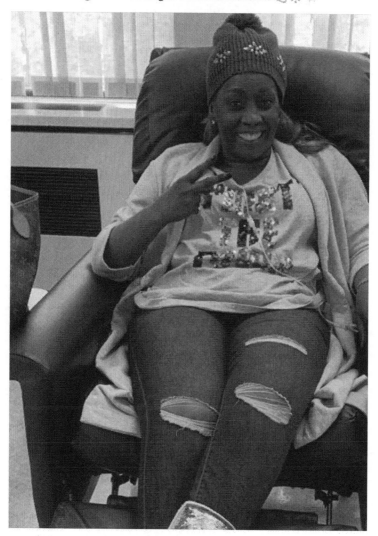

Taleshia Chandler
March 29 at 5:50 PM · 🌐   •••

Heyyy! So, I started off my day having a little pity party because... my hand was hurting (neuropathy); I had a difficult time putting my earrings on; oh yeah, couldn't button my top 😳; I have no eyebrows; no eyelashes...then, I realized that I still have hands; my feet hurt, but I can walk; I can see; I went to school for makeup art years ago just for fun...so I know how to create brows and apply la... See More

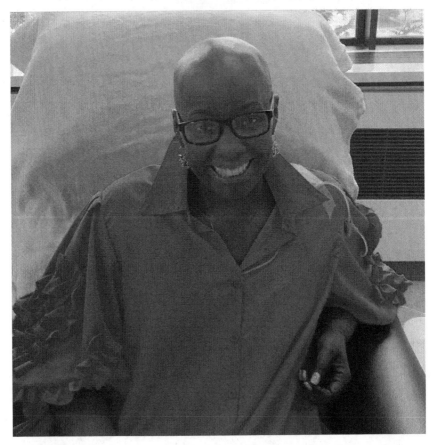

⭕💙😢 726   253 Comments 1 Share

👍 Like   💬 Comment   ➤ Share

doctlc   •••

❤ 💬 ✈   🔖

🐾🐾🐾 Liked by **mrsnyibe** and **107 others**

doctlc Happy Friday!!! #adivinedetour

5

When Jesus heard that, he said, This sickness is not unto death, but for the glory of God, that the Son of God might be glorified thereby. – John 11:4

ANSWERING "HOW DO YOU DO IT?" SEVEN KEYS TO ACTIVATING YOUR SPARKLE MENTALITY

Hopefully, by this point, you're sold on the benefits that sparkling through adversity can have both on your life and the lives of others. If so, you are now ready to begin activating your sparkle mentality. There are seven keys that are necessary for activating the mentality that you need to begin sparkling through adversity. As you can probably guess, these keys are all associated with helping you to look your best every single day so that you can do your best and be your best, resulting in you feeling your best. When you feel your best, you shine brightly for all the world to see. When they see you sparkling in the midst of your adversity, they can't help but be inspired – and impressed!

The seven keys to activating your sparkle mentality include the following:

 ⋆ Key 1: Get out of bed
 ⋆ Key 2: Dress your best
 ⋆ Key 3: Put on some makeup
 ⋆ Key 4: Smell good
 ⋆ Key 5: Style your hair, buy some hair or rock it bald!
 ⋆ Key 6: Eat well
 ⋆ Key 7: Smile

Key 1: Get Out of Bed

First things first: no matter how bad you feel, you've *got* to get out of the bed – unless you're confined to the bed by doctor's orders, of course. In that case, stay in bed for as long as you've been ordered to be on bed rest. All others, get out of bed! I know that you might feel too mentally and physically drained to throw back those warm, cozy covers and put your feet on the floor, but you've got to make yourself do it. I know that all you really want to do is lay there and focus on your misery, think about all of the questions you have that remain unanswered, forecast all of the dreadful things that the future might hold for you, and just be alone. However, if you're going to sparkle through your adversity, it begins with getting out of bed, no matter how sad or bad you feel.

I know that getting out of bed when you're going through adversity isn't easy. Remember: I've had plenty of adversity of my own. In the beginning, I would stay in bed all day long. It's not that I was sleeping, because I had full-blown insomnia both day and night. I was just lying there focusing on my questions, my sadness, and my aches and pains. It's not until I activated my sparkle mentality that I pulled myself out of bed and started focusing on looking, doing, and being my best, and making the most of every day. Even now, some mornings are quite difficult because I'm in lots of pain. It takes several minutes to plant my feet on the floor, but I do it!

There is a world out there just waiting for you to enjoy, if you're bold enough to get out there and enjoy it. There are people out there just waiting to give you hugs of love, to listen to you, and to provide you with support, if you simply come out of the isolation of your bedroom. Staying in your bed for extended hours outside of your normal bedtime can trap you in a sunken place full of pity and darkness. When you choose to stay in this place, you cut yourself off from interacting with people who can motivate you and whom you can inspire. Never forget that you and your story will serve as the inspiration that will change people's lives... and it all begins with the first step: getting out of bed!

Key 2: Dress Your Best

When I was about to go to my first chemotherapy session after I was diagnosed with cancer, in my mind, I was dressed for the occasion. I threw on some sweat pants, t-shirt, and tennis shoes, and I was about to head out the door to go to this cancer center that I did not want to go to at all. I admit it. I looked a mess... like I was about to go do some laundry. When my husband saw me, he looked at me and said, "Uh, uh! Oh, no! I *know* you're not going out of here like *that!*" You see, my husband knows me. He knows that I love makeup, I always have my nails done, and that I always like to wear nice things. He said, "Don't let cancer change who you are." Then, he went on to explain to me that he wanted me to look my absolute best every time I went to my chemotherapy sessions. In fact, he said that he wanted me to look so good that when I went to the cancer center and sat in the waiting room, he didn't even want people to be able to look at me and know that I was a patient. Any other time that I went outside of the house, I was in a nice outfit, full makeup, and completely pulled together, so why stop now? His final piece of advice was one that he knew would resound with me, because I would know exactly the look he wanted: "Dress like you're going to the mall."

Honestly, my husband's words irritated me at first. However, I knew full well that I looked a hot mess, so I couldn't blame him for sending me back to the drawing board, which was my closet. I changed my outfit and put some makeup on and then came back out to re-present myself to him for approval. When my husband saw me, he said, "Yes! Now, that's my wife! That's the way I want you to always look. I don't want you to lose who you are just because you have cancer." With that, we headed to the cancer center. I can honestly admit that as I rode in the car that day to my very first chemo treatment, my wardrobe change and fresh lipstick did make me feel much better about myself than I did before.

I share this story with you so that you understand that I did not start where I am today. It was a process for me, just like it's going to be a process for you. The point is that you be willing to engage in the process and move from your drab, dull mentality to a sparkle mentality. Remember: sparkling through adversity is not only for your benefit but for the benefit of others, adding inspiration to their lives.

From that first day on, I did just as my husband advised: I dressed my best. Sometimes, I would even put on lashes and a full face of makeup, looking like I was headed to the opera! Every time I would go to the cancer center, I constantly received compliments from the nurses and technicians. They would say, "Oh my goodness, you look so nice!" Even as time went on and cancer began taking its toll on my body, I would still show up dressed my absolute best. The cancer center staff, who read my charts, knew my cell counts, and were aware of how critical my situation was, would be shocked each time they saw me. They would say, "You don't even look like you belong here in the patient center!" and "If I didn't already know for myself what was going on with you, there is no way that I'd be able to tell that you're a cancer patient!" However, my favorite feedback is that which I would get from the other cancer patients when I went to chemo. When they would say things to me like, "Wow, you look great! Next time, I'm gonna dress up and put my makeup on, too!" I knew that I was touching and inspiring lives with my sparkle. Although I did not originally set out to get such a response from the people at the cancer center – I'd just done it because my husband told me to – I really appreciated the impact that my sparkle was having on other people.

Key 3: Put on Some Makeup (for Ladies)

When you look good, you feel much better about yourself, and nothing makes you look better in only a few minutes than makeup. I absolutely love makeup! I love it for so many reasons. It makes me feel pretty, it makes me feel feminine, it makes me feel polished… it's just the best! I've been dealing with cancer for four years now, so my face bears the evidence of it. My once-flawless skin now has some discoloration and scars. When I look into the mirror, especially without any hair, I feel like there's a little boy looking back at me. However, my husband always encourages me, saying, "No! You look beautiful!" That's why it's so important to have the right people around you. I love that man!

Don't get me wrong. To be clear, I love myself and feel good about myself without makeup. However, I just love how makeup boosts my confidence and makes me feel even better about myself. It also makes me feel more comfortable when I go out of the house and interact with other people. I'm not as self-conscious about what my cancer journey has done to my skin, and I feel like people are looking at me instead of trying to figure out what happened to my skin. Fortunately, I happen to be really good at applying makeup and making myself look my absolute best. In fact, I can handle makeup like a pro!

It's so crazy the way God works things out in life. He always sets you up for what you need. I say this because back when I was still living in Baltimore and was pregnant with my oldest son, I loved makeup so much that I decided to get my makeup license. I was still a teacher at the time, so after I completed the course and got my license, I decided that I would work as a makeup artist during the summer after school ended. I was privileged to work at some of the best makeup counters, like Chanel and MAC. There, I learned all the secrets of applying makeup like a pro, and I also got a lot of practice using the customers. Over time, however, I realized that I loved makeup, but I only loved doing my own makeup – not other people's makeup. It was at that point that I stopped working at department store makeup counters and began just doing my own makeup.

Little did I know that the makeup training and experience that I had gained years before would come in so handy later in life. Today, even though the chemo has taken my eyebrows and eyelashes, I can create my eyebrows and apply my own lashes. When I'm on steroids and my face looks swollen and bloated, I can use makeup contouring on my face so that I can look and feel like my normal self. I'm grateful for these valuable skills, because they allow me to start every day with a positive outlook, simply because of the way I look!

Key 4: Smell Good

You might think that it goes without saying that a person should smell good in order to activate the sparkle, but that's simply not so. A lot of people who close themselves off from the world, stay in bed all day, and withdraw from life because of adversity do not feel the need to keep themselves clean and smelling good. As they wallow in their dark place, they might go for days at a time without showering or brushing their teeth. When you do not make a deliberate effort to smell good, it is almost as if you're saying that you don't want people around you and that you want to stay alone in your sunken place, lost and alone. However, smelling good is not an option if you're going to sparkle through adversity. Remember, sparkling with adversity means getting back out and engaging with the world. On behalf of the world, I would like to encourage you to first bathe, put on some deodorant, and brush your teeth. Sparkling and smelling bad do not go together!

Another level of smelling good, beyond that of basic hygiene, is putting on some perfume or cologne. I consider perfume and cologne and mood a cyclical relationship. I can say from personal experience that sometimes when I'm not feeling my best, all it takes is putting on some of my favorite perfume, almost instantly, my mood lifts. I feel happier, prettier, more confident, and eager to get out into the world to interact with others and enjoy life.

When I smell people wearing nice perfume or cologne, it communicates to me that they feel good about themselves. I mean, think about it. People who don't feel good about themselves are just going to throw something on and not care about how they look or smell. However, people who do feel good about themselves are going to be deliberate in their choice of what to wear, and they complement looking nice with smelling nice. They are intentional about drawing others to themselves by spraying on some perfume or cologne because they want people to notice and say, "He smells really nice," or "She smells so good." They feel so good about themselves that they want other people to notice how good they look and smell!

Therefore, after you ensure that you smell good through exercising basic hygiene, go the extra mile to enhance it by using perfume and cologne. Not only will smelling good make you feel good about yourself, but it will also make others feel good about you, and it will communicate to them that you feel good about yourself. It's all a win-win!

Key 5: Style Your Hair, Buy Some Hair or Rock It Bald!

When my oncologist first diagnosed me with stage 4 breast cancer, the first question that came out of my mouth was, "Am I going to lose my hair?" It was like a reflexive response. You would think that my immediate first concern would be about my prognosis. However, it didn't occur to me to first ask him if the cancer was going to take my life or if I was going to have to undergo chemotherapy. Instead, it was all about my hair.

I share this story with you so that you can know how serious of a matter my hair was for me. Before I got cancer, I had a hair ritual. Every single Friday, like clockwork, I would go to the hair salon to get my hair professionally done. I had a standing appointment to sit in my stylist's chair and let her whip my hair into a fresh style that would keep me looking my best. It was relaxed and straight back then, and because of my weekly appointments, it was always healthy, bouncy and beautiful. It was a part of my identity; I felt it was a part of what made me who I was. In response to my question, my doctor explained to me that with the chemotherapy drug he was putting me on, most of his patients either lost their hair, or their hair became extremely thin. True to his words, this is exactly what happened to me after I began chemotherapy.

It was very hard in the beginning. I would be standing in the mirror styling my hair, and clumps of my hair would come out in the comb. I could just be running my fingers through my hair, and there would be clumps of hair in my hand. Pretty soon, I decided that instead of enduring a long, painful loss of my beloved hair, I would take action: I had my stylist cut it all off. I went with a very short haircut, and rather than relaxing it into straightness, I kept it natural. This wasn't an easy thing to do! In fact, it was one of the hardest things that I have ever had to do and face.

I thought that I had nipped things in the bud by speeding up the process and cutting all of my hair off, but as it turns out, that wasn't the end of it. I was growing accustomed to my short, curly natural hair. It was different from any hairstyle I'd ever had, but it was my new normal. I asked, "God, I can live with this. Can you please let it stay just like this?" I guess His answer was "No." The little hair that I still had on my head started coming out again. I was so afraid that I would be completely bald that some days, I literally wouldn't comb my hair; I felt like if I didn't comb it, I would be able to keep it. Of course, it didn't take long for it to all fall out. I was completely bald. I simply couldn't believe that this was happening to me.

At first, I was so devastated at my baldness that I tried to cover my head. I tried wearing wigs, thinking that they might be a good solution. However, the wigs made me itch, and they were really uncomfortable, so they didn't work for me. One day, I stood in the mirror and I had an important conversation with myself. I said, "Look, Taleshia. You have cancer. Your hair is falling out because you're in chemo. This is where you are at this point. You're still alive, you're still beautiful, and anything you put on, you know how to rock. So instead of covering up this bald head, just *rock it*, girl!" From that day on, I tossed the wigs aside and simply rocked my beautiful bald head.

I was on the church praise team at the time that chemo led to the loss of all my hair. The day that I decided to rock my bald head in public for the very first time was a Sunday – of all days! I didn't tell anyone in advance. I put on a nice outfit, made up my face, put on my lashes, shined my bald head, and went to church. My husband and I drive to church separately on Sunday mornings, because he has to be at church earlier and hang around after-wards later than I do, so this first public appearance of my bald head was going to be a surprise to everyone – including him!

I was still on the church praise team at the time, so when I got to church, I just confidently walked up on the pulpit to join the singers like it was any other day. It wasn't until a couple of months later that my husband told me that it was really hard for him to see me that morning, because he never would have thought that I would come to church bald. However, that morn-ing that he saw me stride into the church with my bald head, he thought I was so beautiful. He told me that what sold the look was my confidence; I had walked in with such an attitude that it just made people immediately accept it rather than question it! His words, and the positive affirmation from others who com-mented on my beautiful, bald look that day and thereafter really helped me during this season. One of the things that made me smile the most was when my girlfriends would say to me, "Well, at least you have a nicely-shaped head! Everybody doesn't have the kind of head shape to be bald!" They were right, and I really am grateful for the little things. Thank God that He blessed me with a head that still looks cute without hair.

This brings me to our fifth key: make your hair look nice, and if you don't have any hair, rock it bald! Whatever you do, be in-tentional about working whatever's on your head so that it's your best. If you have hair of any length, appreciate it! There are some people who don't have hair who wish they had your hair! If you have long hair, style it and make it look good. You don't have to go to a professional like I used to do, but do all you can to make sure that it's nice and styled. If you have short hair, whether it's natural or relaxed, keep it cute. If you're bald, whether because of cancer, alopecia, or any other reason, shine your head and rock it with boldness and confidence! I'm a living witness that you can be off-the-charts cute without any hair. The bottom line is, whatever you have (or don't have) on your head, rock what you've got, and do your absolute best to make it look nice! Recently, I've started wearing a lace wig to keep my head warm!

At the end of the day, the most important thing is that you like what you see when you look in the mirror while you're going through adversity. In fact, liking what you see when you look at yourself in the mirror each morning could be the first step towards your healing and enduring your situation with style and grace. I promise that you'll like what you see more if you put in a little effort to make your head look its best. It will fill you with a whole new sense of confidence and expectation as you go out and interact with the rest of the world in the middle of what you're going through in life.

Although losing my hair was one of my greatest nightmares in life, I'm sparkling through my adversity just like my bald head is. It sparkles and shines in the sunlight, and I couldn't be more proud. I'm not sensitive about it at all; it's a testament to what I'm going through and how I'm going through it – with boldness, style and grace. I'm not hiding who I am in the midst of my adversity; I'm letting it shine, shine, shine! I'm even at the point where I can make jokes with my friends about my bald head.

I can recall one instance when I went on a girls' trip with a few of my girlfriends. When we got to the hotel room, I was ready to take a shower. I went in the bathroom for a few seconds, and then I walked back out and said, "Oh, no! I didn't bring my shower cap! Does anybody have a shower cap?" At once, they all began looking through their suitcases to loan me a shower cap. It was such a funny sight to see! Finally, I was like, "Y'all know I don't really need a shower cap, right? I'm *bald!*" With that, we all cracked up laughing, and I went back into the bathroom to take my shower. That was only one of several jokes about my bald head that I use with my friends. I'll also joke about how I can't go out into the rain, because I'll get my hair wet.

I can't lie. I miss my hair – *all* of it. The hair on my head, my eyebrows, my lashes, everything. However, neo-soul songstress, India.Arie, has a song entitled "I Am Not My Hair," and the lyrics fit how I feel about my hair to a tee. I really am *not* my hair. Having hair does not define me, so not having hair doesn't change the definition of who I am. I'm still the same person, whether my hair is long and flowing, short and natural, or completely gone. Sometimes my hair grows back a little when I'm on a milder chemo medicine, and I'll color my soft, new baby curls a bright, eye-catching platinum blond! Other times, my doctor will switch me to a stronger chemo medicine that causes my cute little hair to fall out again. Either way, I refuse to be down or depressed about it. Whatever the good Lord allows me to have at any given time, I'm going to rock it with boldness, with confidence and with an attitude that shouts to the world, "Look at me, cancer and all, and watch me sparkle through this thing like a boss!"

Key 6: Eat Well

You're probably expecting this key to be filled with suggestions on cutting out the sugar, carbs and fat and eating only lean proteins and lots of green, leafy vegetables so that you can be super healthy. Well, you can let your guards down now, because I'm not going to do that. When I say that you should eat well, I am saying that you should eat in such a way that you are taking care of yourself. You know what your body needs. You know if you eat a balanced diet or not. You know if your body is healthy and strong enough to get you through whatever you're going through or not. Eat enough of the food you need so you can have the energy to sparkle through your adversity, because sparkling takes energy; you can't sparkle if you're weak and on the verge of fainting all the time. Therefore, continue eating a diet that you know is most suitable for keeping up your energy and that you can keep up with, considering your current lifestyle.

When I was first diagnosed with stage 4 breast cancer, of course, I was like a lot of people: I thought that everything about my diet had to change in order for me to beat the disease. In my own logic, I had concluded that the reason I was diagnosed with cancer in the first place, other than negligent doctors at the time, was because of how I ate. I thought that I was going to have to stop eating red meat, sugar, and all of the other good stuff that I love, and the thought of cutting all of the delicious foods I love saddened me. However, the first time that I had an appointment with my current oncologist, I was shocked. One of the first things that he said to me during the visit was, "Taleshia, I know that this is difficult, but the first thing I want you to do is *not* drastically change your diet. Don't change the way you're eating."

My doctor explained that when most people hear that they have cancer, they want to start doing all of this holistic stuff and switch to a healthier diet. His advice was to do the opposite: don't switch things around. He gave me instructions to keep eating what I'd always been eating and to keep myself hydrated. Most of all, he told me to keep plenty of water in order to flush my system and to not get dehydrated. My doctor knew that as long as I kept eating my same diet, I could keep up the strength that I needed to be able to handle the treatments and drugs that I was about to start putting in my body. He cautioned me not to allow this situation to cause me to cut back on what I ate, but he also warned me not to overeat, because he didn't want me to have a dramatic weight increase. There was a reason for this. Each time I went for a chemotherapy treatment, the amount of chemo drugs that they gave me was based on how much I weighed. At every chemo appointment, they weighed me first so that they would know the proper amount of drugs to give me. The more you weigh, the more the amount of drugs you need, and the less you weigh, the lesser the amount of drugs you need. With all of these things in mind, I followed my doctor's orders. I didn't make any drastic changes to my diet, I didn't undereat or overeat, and I made sure that I consistently ate well so that I could keep my strength up so I would have the opportunity to get well.

Whatever you do, don't stop eating. I know that when you're going through the most devastating situations of your life, they can rob you of your appetite. Fight the urge to go all day without eating. Stay consistent. If you normally ate breakfast, lunch and dinner before your season of adversity, make yourself continue eating breakfast, lunch and dinner while you're going through. Remember, you can't sparkle through your situation if you're looking frail and weak. You can't get through your storm with style and grace if you don't have enough energy to get out of bed and walk across the room without getting lightheaded. Don't let the trauma that you're experiencing steal what you need to fuel your sparkle. You need food, so make sure you eat well.

Recently, my family experienced several difficult traumatic events at the same time. We lost my grandmother, I had a really serious health scare, and the week of my grandmother's funeral, my nephew had a serious accident. My mother is the backbone of our family, a strong, caring woman who sees to the well-being of everyone. As you can imagine, dealing with the loss of her mother, the critical health crisis of her daughter, and the life-threatening situation of her grandson was a lot to bear all at once. Although she is a woman of great faith, she was dealing with grief, mixed with concern, mixed with fear and uncertainty – all at the same time. That's a lot for anyone to deal with, even if they do have a strong relationship with God.

The way that my mother dealt with all of these traumas happening at the same time was she stopped eating. Literally. There was so much going on with her emotions and trying to mentally handle all that she was going through that the last thing she could bring herself to do was eat. She had no appetite at all. In fact, she passed out in her kitchen. Fortunately, my sister was there with her at the time, so she was able to help her. As soon as my sister got my mom up, she called me on FaceTime so that I could see my mom and talk to her. My sister had begged my mother to eat something, but she simply wouldn't eat. She knew that my mom listened to me, so she called me hoping that I could convince her to eat something. As soon as I saw my mom's face on my phone screen, I was shocked and immediately concerned. This was serious. I knew that she'd been having a hard time with all that had been going on, but before that point, I didn't realize she'd stopped eating. She'd lost so much weight that she looked ill. I could tell just by looking at her that she was out of it. She'd been starving herself!

I begged and pleaded with my mother to eat something. She kept saying she was fine and that she wasn't hungry. No matter what I said, she wouldn't agree to eat a thing. Then, I pulled a punch that I knew would get her: I told her that until she ate something, I was going to completely stop eating, too, and I was going to stop taking my medicine. That was all she needed to hear. She said, "No!" The thought of her daughter doing what she was doing to herself was more than she could handle. She finally agreed to have something to eat. My sister stayed with her and watched as she ate a piece of toast and drank a soda. It wasn't much, but it was a start. We stayed on top of her until we were sure that she was at least eating something every day.

The funny thing is, before this, I really didn't realize that people dealt with things by not eating! To stop eating when you're going through something was not what I had experienced or heard of before. Me, I eat more when I'm going through something. I feed my feelings with food as a way of coping. Many of my friends are the same way; they want to eat more when they are going through stressful or devastating situations. The point in all of this is that no matter what you are inclined to do – eat more or eat less – you should remain consistent. Don't allow your trauma to dramatically alter the way you eat. Instead, make sure that you eat well so that you can keep up your strength for the journey and the energy that you need to keep sparkling!

Key 7: Smile

If you've ever seen the Broadway musical "Annie," you've no doubt heard the saying, "You're never fully dressed without a smile!" It's actually the title of a song that the cast sings in the show. Guess what? They're right! You can put on all the right clothes, put on heels or other nicely-shined shoes, do your hair, put on a face of full makeup and some lashes, and spray on some of your favorite cologne or perfume. However, if you walk around looking like a star in each of these areas but wear a frown or a scowl on your face, people will disregard the message that you're trying to communicate through your outfit, your impeccable makeup job, and your nicely-coiffed hair (or shiny bald head). All they'll be able to pay attention to is how sad and down you look. This is because your facial expression speaks volumes to others, and it speaks loudly!

Always keep the mission in mind. I'm trying to teach you how to sparkle through your adverse situation, and there are several aspects of sparkling through adversity that require a smile. For example, Aspect 4 of the sparkling through adversity mindset says that "You dare to still fully enjoy life, despite your devastating circumstances." How better to communicate that you're still enjoying life than to show it with a smile? When you walk around with a negative expression, what you're communicating to the world is that your devastating circumstances are getting the best of you. Then, Aspect 7 of the sparkling through adversity mindset says that "You live a life filled with faith, trust in God, and hope rather than a life of fear, worry and doom." If you asked someone what each one of these expressions looked like, I guarantee that they would say that a person who lives a life of fear, worry and doom would have a sad, pitiful expression, and a person who lives with faith, trust in God, and hope would carry an expression of peace, calm, and happiness – a smile! Therefore, when you're not wearing a smile, you're not being intentional about sparkling through your adversity. More significant than that, you're witnessing to the world that God can put a smile on your face, even during the worst of times.

There's also another saying about smiles that I'm sure you've heard of before: it takes more facial muscles to frown that it does to smile. I'm not sure if this is true or not, because even though it's a commonly-accepted notion, it's unproven. In this case, let's assume it is true; after all, everyone else does! Considering that fighting through your trauma takes a significant amount of energy, why use up the little energy that you have left by frowning? Smiling is physically easier, takes less energy, and can help you to reflect God's goodness in your life, even when you're going through something traumatic.

I'm sure you might be thinking, "Does this mean that I'm supposed to always be happy? There's no way that I can keep a smile pasted on my face with all of the stuff that I'm going through!" The answer to your question is "No." I don't expect for you to always be happy. Heck, I'm not even happy all the time. Some days, I just really need a good cry. Do you know what I do on those days? I cry! I cry and cry until I get it all out of my system, and then I wipe my face, thank God for His grace to keep on going, and keep it moving… with a smile. Don't let people who are not going through what you're going through try to convince you that if you cry in the middle of your adversity, you don't have faith and trust in God, you are being a poor witness, or that you're showing weakness. Crying is a natural response to experiencing life-changing trauma. However, the important thing is to not allow yourself to stay in that state of sadness. Once you get your cry out, clean yourself back up and move on in faith.

Here's another reason that you should smile: it makes you feel better! This happens because putting on an intentional smile tricks the body into thinking that you're happy. Then, your body releases endorphins – also known as the "feel good hormone" – on the inside. Think about it: even if you're sad, when you smile, your body literally *drugs* itself with a substance that makes you feel much better than you did before you began to smile. It's a biological fact (now, this one *is* proven by research)! When you understand this, you realize that you can physically shift your mood by simply choosing to stretch up the corners of your mouth into a big ol' grin!

Finally, one of the best reasons to smile is that it attracts people to you rather than repelling them from you. There are two types of people who are affected by your smile. First is your support group. As much as you might want to be alone as you struggle through your adversity, you must face reality: you *need* people. Period. I know that you, with your independent, individualist spirit, feel like you can do anything you want to do all by yourself and often want to be left alone. However, if you're going to sparkle through adversity, you can't do it alone. Sparkling through adversity is something that you do as you are empowered by a network of people who support you, and you do a disservice to these people when you choose to always walk around full of gloom and doom.

Second, onlookers are going to be affected by your smile. Your ability to wear a smile despite what you're going through makes you approachable to other people – the kind of approachable that makes people feel comfortable walking up to you to say things like, "You really encourage me!" or "I know your situation, and watching how you're going through this with a smile is incredible! You truly inspire me," or "Your life is such an amazing witness about how God can keep a person during a storm!" If they don't walk up and speak to you, sometimes they will just smile at you to let you know that they see you... smiling and sparkling!

When you smile, you are inviting the world to interact with you. However, the opposite is true, too. When you are looking sad and down, you are sending a subconscious message to people telling them to keep their distance. If you're kind of in-between – you're neither smiling nor frowning – your mood is harder to read. In these cases, people usually err on the safe side and choose not to approach and interact with you. They don't want to take the chance on saying the wrong thing, doing the wrong thing, bothering you, upsetting you, or making you sadder, especially in light of what you're already going through.

Never forget that the goal of sparkling through adversity is to attract people into your space, not drive them out of it. Therefore, do your best to make them feel as comfortable as possible in approaching you by simply smiling. It's such a small thing to do, but it makes such a big impact on others. When people know your story and the adverse situation that you're going through and they see you still smiling as you go through it, you're sending a clear message: you're sparkling through adversity!

6

Now faith is the substance of things hoped for, the evidence of things not seen. – Hebrews 11:1

THE SPARKLING THROUGH ADVERSITY PACKING LIST: WHAT TO BRING ALONG ON THE JOURNEY OF A LIFETIME

Adversity is like a bad house guest. It's not that warm, pleasant house guest that comes to town bearing gifts, cooks you a delicious gourmet dinner, stays overnight, and leaves first thing in the morning. Instead, adversity is that unwelcomed, unpleasant, obnoxious, and demanding house guest that lingers, disrupts your life, and never seems to want to leave. Adversity hangs around for a while. If it were to simply come and go quickly, it wouldn't have such life-changing, devastating effects. That's what makes it so challenging. Adversity is not a day... it's a season. It's not a moment in time... it's a journey that you have to get through day by day.

When you hear the word "journey," what probably comes to your mind is a very long trip that takes you to unknown places and that is filled with new, unexpected experiences. If you've ever been on a travel journey, you know that they can be lots of fun. Journeys fill our hearts and mind with experiences that we never, ever forget. However, journeys can be good – like the extended vacation adventure that you took to a Caribbean island – or they can be bad, trying and challenging. When you're on your journey through adversity, you're dealing with the latter. An adversity journey is a different type of journey. In fact, I can confidently say that journeys through adversity are the most unforgettable journeys that you'll ever take in your life.

Everybody who knows me knows that I love to travel. I get so excited about going on a new adventure, especially when it's an unexpected surprise! My husband is known for surprising me by saying, "We're going on a trip!" and all of a sudden, I'm filled with anticipation of what's to come. I get so happy... I can't wait to pull out my luggage and prepare for the trip! Fortunately, I'm a seasoned traveler; we've journeyed to all kinds of fun places. Over the years, I've gained some valuable experience on how to pack for the journey ahead. I'm so good at packing, I can do it with my eyes closed. I can easily advise you on how to pack for any journey – cold weather journeys, warm weather journeys, unpredictable weather journeys, island journeys, cruise journeys... you name it!

Because I am such an expert on how to pack for a journey, I thought I would answer the question that so many people have asked me – the "How do you manage to go through your adversity with such style and grace?" question – by sharing with you about how I pack for the journey. Again, adversity is not a quick trip; it's a long journey. You can expect to be away from your "normal life" for a while. It's a season that seems like it's never going to end, so how you pack and what you pack for the trip are critical to being able to get through it properly. If you don't bring the right things along on the journey, yes, you'll still get through the journey. However, you won't get through it with as much comfort, peace, and elegance as you would if you pack the right things for the journey. It's like the difference between flying first or business class and flying coach for a 10-hour international trip. Regardless of your seat class, you're all going to get to the same destination, but I guarantee, one is a much more stylish and comfortable experience than the other.

What follows is a very special packing list of 10 things that you'll need to be sure you bring along. Each of the items will help you get through your journey of adversity with style and grace. These things are designed to help you sparkle through your adversity so that, along your journey, people can't help but stop you and ask, "What's your secret? How are you getting through this so well?" If you take heed to my expert packing advice, you'll be sparkling through your own adversity so brightly that people won't be able to help but take notice and ask you how you do it, too!

Here's the Ultimate Sparkling through Adversity packing list:
1. A Carry-On Bag of "Essentials"
2. A Pair Of Sunglasses with "Gratitude-Colored" Lenses
3. Your Best, "Sparkliest" Attire and Accessories
4. A Really Good Camera with a Sharp, Manual-Focus Lens
5. A Daily Itinerary
6. A Mirror that Shows You the "Real You"
7. Great Travel Companions
8. "Grace Passes" for the Not-So-Well Behaved
9. A Journal
10. Meds

Item 1: A Carry-on Bag of "Essentials"

By far, one of the most important things that you should bring along for a long journey is your carry-on bag filled with essentials. Your essentials are the things that you simply can't live without. They are items that are so important, you won't even place them in your checked luggage, because you want to keep them with you at all times. Your essentials are things that you will need to be able to access immediately throughout any point of your journey, because they all play a major role in your peace, comfort and happiness. In doing so, they help you sparkle through your journey with style and grace.

What goes into your carry-on bag of essentials will vary from person to person and from journey to journey. So that you can get a better idea of must-haves that you should bring along on your journey, here's a glimpse of what's in my carry-on bag of essentials:

* GOD – By far, the most important essential in my carry-on bag is God. I have to keep Him with me at all times in order to not only survive but sparkle through the journey.

* PRAYER – It's not enough just to have God with me; I realize that I have to talk to Him throughout the day every day. It makes no sense to have Him and ignore Him! I make sure that I not only keep Him close but that I check-in with Him, share what's on my heart with Him, and ask Him to guide me on my journey.

* THE BIBLE – The Bible is God's Word, so when I read it, it is God speaking back to me, giving me the guidance and direction that I need on my journey. Reading my Bible helps me to remember His promises and trust Him more when things get hard along the way.

* FAITH – I bring my faith along as a must-have that I can access at any point on my journey, especially when fear, worry and doubt try to creep in, telling me that I'm not going to make it. My faith helps me to look at God and the eternal things that I cannot see instead of looking at the odds that are stacked up against me on the journey.

* FRIENDS – Friendships matter to me and are so important along my journey. I keep them close and accessible so that whenever I need them, I can reach out to them for a listening ear, a word of encouragement, or a good laugh.

* LAUGHTER – If I'm not laughing, I'm not living! I *love* to laugh and have a good time! Laughter is a non-negotiable for me. I need to be able to access something or someone who can make me laugh when I need it most. My greatest laugh-makers are my friends. They make me laugh by sending me funny videos, silly text messages, and fun-

ny memes. These, and the laughter they bring, make the darkest days of my journey much brighter.

* TRAVEL – Out of all my hobbies, travel is one that I love the most. I love it so much that it isn't something that I just want to do; I need travel as a part of my life! Fortunately, my husband is like an undercover travel agent; he finds the best deals, and then he just comes home and announces, "We're going on a trip!" My most favorite trips that he takes me on are cruises. I love the food, the activities, the relaxation, and the fact that once you get on the cruise ship, everything is taken care of and paid for already. However, travel of any type replenishes in me so much of what my journey through adversity takes out of me, so I consider it an essential, must-have part of my life.

* WORK – Most people would never put work on their list of essentials to keep close by so they can access it immediately. However, I love my job – a lot! It gives me purpose. I actually can't wait to wake up every day and go to my job as an assistant principal working with students with disabilities. Work is a way for me to dig into my job helping students and mentoring teachers, and thankfully, this takes my mental focus off of everything going on with my health.

* CHURCH – Some might consider going to church to be in the same category as God and faith, but to me, they are totally different. Church is a necessity that I've *got* to have access to on my journey. A lot of times, when people go through adverse situations, they stop going to church. They say, "I'm going through something right now, but I'll be back once I get myself together." I might be biased because my husband is a pastor, but I believe that church should be a place that you go to in order to find the strength that you need on your journey. I find strength in the preaching, the music, and the fellowship with others. I also consider church a necessity because it's one place where, after a really difficult week, I can go to have a good cry. I'm able to leave all of the pain, frustration and negativity on the

altar and leave with a positive boost of energy that helps me to get through the next week. Sometimes, when my husband sees that I'm not doing well on a church day, he'll say, "Why don't you just stay home and get some rest today? You can just watch the service online." I always say, "No." Watching online is not the same. I can only feel the positive energy and gain the strength that I need when I'm in God's house, in His presence. That's why, for me, going to church is not a want; it's a real need.

* SELF-CARE – Paying attention to what you need as an individual is not optional when you're on a difficult journey; it's essential. I can't be there for others if I'm not taking care of myself. Self-care simply involves cutting away from doing for everyone else in order to do things for me. Sometimes, this means recording my favorite game shows, and then closing my door and watching "Let's Make a Deal" and "The Price is Right" for hours. Other times, it means going out to get a manicure and pedicure. These might be considered small things, but they make me feel cared for in a big way.

* "NO" – As a wife, mother, first lady, friend, daughter, and caretaker in general, it's easy to want to ensure that you do all you can to make others happy. However, on my journey, I must be able to say "No," because saying "Yes" all the time will leave me without what I need to get through my journey. If I don't feel up to doing something or simply don't want to do it because it doesn't work for me, I have quick and easy access to my survival word: "No!"

* ONLINE SHOPPING – I used to feel guilty about admitting that I need to be able to shop. However, now, I don't feel guilty about it, and I don't apologize for it anymore. It's part of what I need to make myself feel good. In fact, it makes me feel so good that I refer to it as "retail therapy!" If I'm feeling terrible and want to buy myself an outfit or a pair of shoes, I do it. After all, I get up every morning and go to

work, earn my own money and pay my tithes, so I deserve to be able to do this small thing that I love – and need!

Item 2: A Pair of Sunglasses with "Gratitude-Colored" Lenses

A good, stylish pair of sunglasses is a must-have when you go on any journey. However, the glasses that you should pack for a journey through adversity are not just any old pair of sunglasses. They should have special lenses – gratitude-colored lenses. If you've ever worn a pair of sunglasses you know that whatever color the lenses of the glasses are, that is the color everything appears to be when you look out into the world. In the same way, when you put on your sunglasses with gratitude-colored lenses, you'll be able to see everything in the world with gratitude.

Every day that you are able to wake up and live your life is a day that you should be thankful and happy. You may not be in full health, but you're alive. Your relationship might be on the rocks and falling apart, but you still have a heart to love. Someone significant may have abandoned you, but you're still loved by God. Your money might be running funny, but you're still eating every day and can laugh, smile and enjoy the sunshine for free. No matter how things get, you always have a reason to be grateful. You can either go through your tough situations moping and complaining, or you can go through them with a sense of gratitude. Either way, you have to go through them. Why not enjoy the journey by choosing to see things in a way that leads to a greater sense of appreciation, hope and expectation for a brighter tomorrow? Put your sunglasses on!

My perspective has shifted so much along my journey simply because I have chosen to put on my sunglasses with gratitude-colored lenses. I've noticed an increase in how much I enjoy life because I'm just so thankful for still being alive. This has helped to eliminate a lot of the sadness and angst that I feel from living with cancer. I notice that when I take my glasses off, I see things completely differently. I see all of the negative things – the aches and pains, the sadness and difficulty, the loss of my hair, eyebrows and eyelashes, needles, scans and appointments. However, through my gratitude-colored lenses, I see and feel differently. Everything is beautiful, including me! I'm grateful for my beautiful family, my church, my job and my friends. I'm grateful for my job, tasks, and assignments and excited to get to them each day. I'm grateful for the beauty of the leaves that change colors with the seasons. I'm grateful for how all of these things bring me such great happiness in ways that they never have before.

Even little things like flowers, which I'll admit I've never really liked or paid much attention to until my journey began, bring me happiness. As I'm driving to work in the mornings, they'll catch my eye. As I look at them, I'll be filled with such gratitude and happiness at their beauty. I see them from a new perspective – as God's bright, colorful and unique creations that decorate the world around us and bring smiles to people's faces. That's not to say that I'd like to receive flowers; I'd rather receive a check or a gift card! However, I've learned to appreciate the beauty of so many little things that I once completely ignored before. On New Year's Day, 2019, my father passed away, and my staff sent me some pink roses. There was a time when I would have thought, "I don't even like flowers. Why do people bother to send flowers?!" This time was different. Through my gratitude-colored lenses, these were the most beautiful roses I'd ever seen, and my heart was filled with appreciation.

Item 3: Your Best, "Sparkliest" Attire and Accessories

When you're packing for a journey through adversity, now is not the time to pull out your flip flops; it's time to pull out your heels! It's not the time to pull out your jogging pants; it's time to pull out your vacation *best*! Pack your hottest accessories, your most gorgeous statement pieces… everything that you wear when you really want to get noticed! Remember, the point of sparkling through adversity is not to blend in but to stand out so that others can see, take notice, and draw inspiration from you and your life. Therefore, don't pack bland things that'll make you blend in; pack things that will sparkle and get you *noticed*!

For example, my favorite accessory of all time, which appears often on my journey, is the denim jacket. I have several. I even found one that is bedazzled with rhinestones and pearls all over it, and I absolutely love it! I can dress it up and wear it with dress trousers or dress it down and wear it with sweats. Whenever I wear my denim jackets, instead of wearing the collar down, I wear it up... even though I know a lot of people might wonder, "Why is her collar up?" I just like it like that. The raised collar, along with the rhinestones and pearls, make me sparkle, shine, and stand out wherever I go!

Another wardrobe piece that I just love is a pair of black sequin wide-leg pants that I found (online, of course!). They are amazing, and they always make me stand out in a crowd. In fact, I recently paired these wide-leg pants with my bedazzled denim jacket for an event in Washington, D.C. One of my sorority sisters launched her makeup line in a new venue, and I wanted to look cute and stand out but still be comfortable. The evening's outfit was a success. It was the perfect blend of style and comfort, and I felt great about how I looked, so I had a wonderful time.

Another thing that I'm always sure that I wear on my journey is high heels. People would think that just because I have cancer, I should always be in flat, comfortable shoes. You know, the ones that they call "sensible" shoes. It is true that sometimes, I do wear flats, but they're always really stylish and are dressy enough for a polished outfit. I usually wear flats at work, because as a school administrator, it's hard to keep heels on all day walking the long, concrete hallways of the school. However, when it is time to go to church, on a date night with my husband, to eat and hang out with my friends, to community meetings, or any other opportunity I have to interact with the public, heels it is!

However, there's one word of caution I'd like to offer for when you're packing your wardrobe for the journey: be comfortable. Popular to contrary belief, you can be cute and be comfortable at the same time. I know, because I prove it every day. I learned my lesson about this one day, and it was one that I never forgot. It was a Sunday, and it was going to be a long day because after our two morning worship services, we were going to have a special anniversary service in the afternoon. The dress that I chose to wear that day required me to wear some additional support underneath; the steroids that my doctor had me on had me so swollen that it was difficult to hold my stomach in on my own like I'd always been able to do before. I put some Spanx on under my dress to control the extra curves and then went to church.

Later in the day, at the beginning of the special afternoon service, I started feeling really bad. My back started hurting, and I was feeling really sick. I took some pain medicine, but it didn't help much at all. I felt so uncomfortable, and I was also drowsy from the pain medicine. It was so bad that I wasn't really able to even enjoy the service. Finally, after service ended, I went straight home. As soon as I took off the Spanx, I realized that they were the culprit! I instantly felt better. Since then, I've chosen not to wear things that require me to wear Spanx in order to hold everything in. Now, while I still dress to impress, I make sure that in addition to being cute, I'm also comfortable.

Finally, don't forget to sparkle with your accessories and other embellishments. Choose necklaces, earrings and other jewelry that highlight your outfit and make you look like a star every day. You can even include sparkle in your makeup and other cosmetics. I know that this might sound crazy, I'm addicted to glitter nail polish! I like the way it sparkles when I'm interacting with people and when I'm in front of people holding a microphone. Over time, chemo and cancer medicines have done damage to the skin on my hands, discoloring them and making them leathery. There are also little marks on them from the constant finger pricks I have to get when I go to the doctor. However, when I wear my glitter nail polish, people are so busy looking at my sparkly nails that they don't pay attention to how my hands look. This glitter polish is so important to me, in fact, that I ordered two whole boxes of glitter polish and took them to my nail salon so they could always have my favorite polish when it was time to do my nails. Before then, they only had three or four basic colors, which their clients typically select for the holiday season. Not me. I have my fingernails sparkling all year round!

The point here is that when you're on your journey through adversity, make sure that you're looking your best. Looking your best will have you feeling your best. As you look and feel your best, people will take notice that you are putting in an intentional effort to shine in the midst of what you're going through on your journey. They'll be attracted to you and inspired by you as you sparkle through it all!

Item 4: A Really Good Camera with a Sharp, Manual-Focus Lens

There's a difference between the camera on my iPhone and a fully-loaded professional-grade photographer's camera with a fancy lens. My iPhone can only focus so closely on something. However, a more 'serious' camera can allow you to focus so closely on something from afar that you can still see the tiniest details in the image. The latter – the one that allows you to sharply focus in on things – is the one that you need to bring along on your journey through adversity. Be sure that the lens should be a manual-focus one, because focusing on things is going to be something that is up to you; it's in your control and according to your own will.

The good thing about this journey is that what you focus upon is your choice. You alone have the ability to choose what you will and will not focus on, so be sure that you focus on the right thing. My advice is that you use your sharp, manual-focus lens to focus on the good instead of the bad; things that make you feel joy and happiness instead of things that make you feel sad and depressed. I know this to be true in my own life. When I focus on having cancer, I get sad and depressed. However, when I choose to focus on all of the good that still surrounds me, I have a more positive outlook and approach to life. This positive outlook helps me to appreciate each and every little thing that comes into my path.

For example, because my husband is a pastor, people often want to interact with me after church. Most of the time, they want to say "Hello," or "I'm praying for you," and just greet me for a moment. Before, I wasn't much of a fan of hanging around for such small talk; I used to try to sneak out, unless someone caught me, and then I'd be cordial for a few moments, wishing they'd finish talking soon. Now, I can say that I'm more present when I'm interacting with other people, much more so than I was before my cancer journey began. Interacting with people is more than just a formality now for me. I am genuinely interested in what people are saying and the details of their lives. When I ask them how they're doing, I'm actually interested. I'm not just being polite; I want to know. Instead of focusing on myself, my issues, or what might happen in the future, I enjoy the person sitting before me to the fullest. I no longer take them for granted. I enjoy everything about them – talking to them, sharing with them, saying words to uplift them, laughing with them and enjoying life! More than I ever have in life, I am focusing on, enjoying and genuinely appreciating each and every interaction that I have with my husband, my children, the people in my church, my sorority sisters, my friends... everyone!

Making a deliberate effort to sharply focus my eyes and energies on things that bring me joy also makes my days much more exciting and fulfilling. It takes my mind off of the things going wrong and allows me to focus on all of the things that are going right. I *choose* to focus on what I'm living and experiencing at the moment instead of focusing on things that steal my joy. There aren't a lot of things that I would call "upsides" to having cancer, but after being on my journey, I feel like one of the reasons that God allowed me to have cancer was that He wanted to teach me to slow down and focus on so many things that I took for granted every day. This is definitely an upside.

Finally, it's important for you to use your camera for what it's really for: capturing memories! Even while you're on your journey through adversity, there are *lots* of amazing memories to make along the way every single day! Don't take these opportunities for granted. Look for them. See them. Experience them. Focus all you have on them. Take a mental snapshot of how good they make you feel and how much happiness they bring into your life. You'll need to be able to access these memories in the future on days when things get rough. When you look back at these memories, they'll bring a smile to your face and brighten up your day!

Item 5: A Daily Itinerary

Nobody sets out on a journey or a long trip without an itinerary. An itinerary is something that outlines what you are going to be doing day by day on the journey. On an actual trip, you have the luxury of having a multi-day itinerary that lets you peek ahead of what you're going to be doing tomorrow, the next day, and even a week from now. However, on this journey through adversity, you have no such luxury. All you have access to is a daily itinerary that allows you to look at what's happening today. In light of this, you should be focused on today. Just today. Not tomorrow, not a month from now, but today.

It's easy to look at all of the things that might happen in the future as you are on your journey through adversity. However, all of the time that you spend on what might happen days, weeks or months from now is time and energy that you could have spent making today amazing. Today could be a really great day if you weren't so fixated on what might happen tomorrow. Today could have been the best day ever if you weren't staring off into the distance wondering about what life might be like if things go differently than you want them to tomorrow. Besides, tomorrow isn't guaranteed to anyone. Therefore, since all we're assured of having is today, let's make the most of it.

If you can discipline yourself to just focus on today, you can give today everything you've got. You can take one day at a time, making each day your absolute best day. After all, you don't know what's going to happen down the road, and even if you did, you couldn't control it. Stop stressing about a future that you can't change anyway! It's a waste of mental and emotional energy and focus. Make a decision that every time your mind tries to advance you ahead to tomorrow, you'll hit the brakes and bring your attention back to today's daily itinerary so you can maximize it, getting everything you possibly can out of it.

Item 6: A Mirror that Shows You the "Real You"

There's nothing like wondering what you look like and not having access to a mirror. You're left wondering whether everything looks okay or if something is out of place. If you think that something is not right with your face, your teeth, your hair or your clothes, you can't even interact comfortably with others until you first get to a mirror so that you can see yourself. Not being able to see the real you can be a great source of discomfort. That's why it's always good to bring a travel mirror along... so that you can see yourself – or your face and hair at least.

As you pack for your journey through adversity, it's also important for you to have a mirror. However, this is not just any mirror; it has to be one that can accurately show you your true self – the *real* you. As you are on whatever journey you are on, it is easy to try to shift who you are and how you feel for other people. We know that our loved ones don't want to see us grieving, suffering, in pain, crying, stressed out, or going through anything that makes us feel uncomfortable. Because of this, we often put our game face on, pretending that we're feeling better than we're feeling and doing better than we're doing. We all do it. At some point, though, you need to be able to close the door, look in the mirror, and really get in touch with where you really are and what you're really feeling.

Having a mirror that shows you the real you is all about the importance of self-reflection as you're going through your journey. It's about staying in touch with the real you and not allowing whatever adversity you're experiencing to make you lose yourself. It's about making sure that there's a place you can go to and fully be yourself – the real you – without any pretense. In this place, you shouldn't feel the pressure to wear a game face. You shouldn't have to pretend that you're okay. This is a place where you allow yourself to feel. If you want to cry, you cry. If you want to feel joy, you can feel joy, allowing it to shine through without feeling any guilt.

In this place of self-reflection, where you can see, be, and get in touch with the real you and where you are in your journey, you also don't try to do more than you're capable of doing. Here, you know your limits. When you look in your mirror, for example, you might see that you're only capable of going out of the house and giving people a couple of hours of your time on a particular day. Well, that's who you are and where you are, so accept it. Don't allow people to push you past where you are.

On my own journey, I've had to take my own personal inventory of where I was. For example, as I mentioned before, I just love my church. I enjoy the preaching, I enjoy the people, I enjoy being the first lady... I enjoy it all! However, with cancer, I'm not able to do as much as I used to. There was a time when I was at church more than I was at home. Now, I'm realistic. I understand what I am and what I'm able to give. I had to trim down my ministry involvement to allow myself an opportunity to get more rest and be fully present and energetic when I do attend events. Although I would love to do more, when I look in the mirror and see my real self, I see that this is all that my real self is able to do at the moment.

Item 7: Great Travel Companions

If you've ever gone on a trip with the wrong person before, you know how important it is to bring the right companion along for the journey. Taking the right trip with the wrong person can turn a dream trip into a nightmare! The last thing that you want to do after you do all of that planning and spend all of that money is to have everything ruined by someone who is high maintenance, negative, pessimistic, and a complainer. They can suck all of the fun out of a trip and make you wish you'd never gone in the first place. This is why I advise you to make sure you bring along the right travel companions as you go on your journey through adversity. They'll make all the difference in how much fun you have, how many adventures you experience, and how you come out feeling on the other side of things.

I have been blessed to have some great travel companions along my journey. First, I have my family along for the ride. My husband and our three children are my main support group. They have made this challenging journey so much more bearable than you could ever imagine. My husband, whom I've already introduced you to, is just amazing. He is my greatest protector, my helper, and my constant companion. I've actually nicknamed him "I Got It!" This is because a lot of times when I feel like I have the strength to try to do something around the house, he simply says, "No, I got it!" When I started my journey, he really stepped up and made sure that everything was done around the house, either by him or by the kids. He doesn't allow me to do any type of housework, and he makes sure that I don't tire myself out too much. He won't even allow me to iron my own clothes!

My husband is the most thoughtful person that I know. For my first birthday after my diagnosis, he went all-out in planning a surprise birthday party for me. He even invited my friends and family to come into town from Baltimore to attend. I was completely taken aback and thankful for this thoughtful thing that he did that I cried for at least 10 minutes when I realized what was happening, and then I cried all over again later that night after we got home. My husband will also plan trips for me and the kids, or he'll plan trips and cruises just for us – to be able to get away together alone for rest and replenishment. His thoughtfulness and attention to detail when planning everything out for me just perfectly are a blessing. It always helps to have a thoughtful person along with you on the journey!

Best of all, my husband keeps his finger on the pulse of where our children are while I'm going through my journey. We have three kids. Two are in college, and our youngest is 16. All of them are amazing in their own unique way. Initially, when my husband and I explained that I was about to begin this journey, they cried and were afraid. However, I told them that I was going to beat it and that the best thing that they could do for me was to get nothing but A's and B's in school and make the best decisions possible. That would be the absolute best medicine their Mommy needed to help her get better.

All of our children stepped up in unbelievable ways without me or my husband having to ask them to do anything – they took care of things all on their own. They cleaned the house, took out the trash, did other chores, and always asked me if I needed anything before they went to their rooms. After my two oldest children went to college, leaving my youngest at home – my "baby" took over and tries to do everything for his mother. He's always asking me, "Mommy, you need water? Did you take your medicine?" He won't let me lift a finger either. In fact, as soon as he hears me pull up in my car, he comes outside to pick up any bags or items that I'm bringing into the house. He'll ask, "Mommy, do you have anything in the trunk? Do you need my help?" I'll say, "No, I'm okay, Son. I've got it." Then, he'll insist on taking whatever I have for me anyway. He won't even allow me to carry my own purse into the house. He'll say, "Mom, this purse is too *heavy*! You shouldn't be carrying anything this heavy." Then, he'll carry it into the house. He is the most helpful son I could have asked for, and he does all that he does without expecting anything in return. When I'm blessed to have all of my children at home, they all pitch in to help around the house. My daughter, my mini-me, is my favorite chauffeur and stylist! She is learning to cook and I love that we share many of the same interests! Lastly, she and my oldest "baby" have even helped me glue my wigs on when I choose to wear them. I thank God for my three babies and I'm so blessed and proud to have them on this journey with me.

Whenever our children have questions about me being sick, they don't come to me; they go to my husband. For example, when I lost my hair from the chemo treatments and came home bald, my son, who was 12 at the time, didn't say a word. He just acted like everything was normal and said, "Hey, Mom." However, he did go to my husband and asked him about what had happened. My husband explained the baldness was due to chemotherapy, but that when I got well, it would grow back. My guess is that my sweet, sweet son, who is very sensitive to taking care of his mother, did not want to risk saying the wrong thing or hurting my feelings by asking about what had happened to my hair. I'm thankful that my husband is always there for him. In fact, my husband regularly does what he calls "Check-ins" with all of our children. From time to time, he'll just call them up to see how they're dealing with the situation and make sure they're okay. He's the best traveling companion a woman could ask for in life!

My husband is not only great at home with the kids, though; he also keeps close watch over me at church. My husband ensures that he reminds people to pray for me, not hug me too hard, and to give me some space so that I don't get too tired out. If I have a negative interaction with someone or someone hurts my feelings, he won't waste a single moment addressing it so that it doesn't happen again. He goes with me to every doctor's appointment. I also have to have an echocardiogram on my heart every three months to make sure that the chemo is not affecting my heart. One time, I had an inappropriate interaction with a male echocardiogram technician. As soon as I told my husband about it, he made sure that he started coming along with me on those appointments, too. Like I said, he's my greatest protector.

Then, there's my mother. She's such a rock in my life. When I'm not doing well, she'll come to my house to stay with us and care for me, and she won't let me lift a finger. She might see me getting up from the couch, and she'll ask, "Where are you going? What are you doing?" Whatever I'm about to do, she's going to make sure that she does it for me. I'll say, "Mom! I'm just going to the restroom!" Then, I think to myself, "I'm 45 years old, and this is my house. I don't have to tell you where I'm going!" I know that she doesn't mean any harm at all by treating me like I'm so fragile. However, sometimes, when she won't let me do anything but rest, I feel like I'm not making a contribution to the household as the lady of the house. I just remind myself that it's all about love. She loves me as strongly as I love my own children. She's just a tad overprotective because she loves me so much. All she wants me to do is focus on resting and getting well.

After I got sick, I began to appreciate my mother at another level. One of the greatest reasons why I appreciate my mother being a traveling companion on this journey with me is because she is a prayer warrior. I can honestly say that if no one else has prayed for me, I know that the reason I'm living right now is because of her prayers. She constantly prays for me, and I know that God hears her prayers. Then, when I call her with good news about positive test results received from the doctor after my scans, as soon as I pick up the phone and say that things are good, she launches into praise, over the phone, for literally 30 minutes (or more). I just sit there listening to her cry and shout thanks and praise to God for keeping her daughter. Once she finally comes back to the conversation, she'll say, "Now, tell me what they said." I'll say another sentence or two about the positive results, and then she'll go back into high praise! This can literally go on for an hour or two. Sometimes, I'll just say, "Mom, I'll call you back a little later," and then hang up, hoping she heard my voice before she heard the dial tone. My mother's prayers for me, fasting for me, and dropping everything to travel into town from Baltimore to be there whenever I'm having a serious procedure make her a priceless travel companion on this journey. I wouldn't want to be on it without her.

Next, my journey would not be the same without my sister, Tabitha, as a traveling companion. I'm the oldest of two siblings; my brother is the middle child, and my sister is the youngest. Even though we are 12 years apart in age, we are quite similar, particularly in our love for music ministry. My sister is a *really* talented full-time professional musician. In addition to being the minister of music at her church, she sings and travels across the world to provide vocals for other artists.

The thing that I love most about my sister is that *nobody* in this world makes me laugh more than her! She is so funny! She has certain catch phrases that she's known for, and once she adopts a saying, she'll use it over and over again in her own unique and hilarious way. For example, one of the things she's known for saying these days is "*Thank* You, Jesus!" It's a simple phrase, but no one can deliver it with the humor, timing, and level of comedic wit than she can. As soon as these words come out of her mouth, I instantly begin bursting into laughter! Another thing that my sister does that completely cracks me up is that she uses animojis, the little animated emojis that you can use to record a message and then send them to someone via text. When the recipient opens the message, the animoji begins talking. Because she knows I love to laugh, my sister will send animojis with *the most* ridiculous, hilarious messages I've ever heard! Of course, as soon as I click on them, I'm doubled over, rolling with laughter.

I appreciate my sister most for her tireless support. She's always been a strong source of support in my life, but after my diagnosis, she was there for me at another level. The first year of my diagnosis, she would make the almost three-hour drive from Baltimore to Richmond for every chemo treatment; she didn't miss a single treatment that whole first year. She would come to Richmond just to sit with me as I went through my treatment. When it was finished and I was all settled, she would then make the drive back to Baltimore. Before I was diagnosed with cancer, we were close, but this experience made us even closer.

Then, there's my mother-in-law, whom I lovingly refer to as "Mother Boobie Dear." Yes, there is a story behind this name! My mother-in-law is a salon owner. Each time one of her clients walked in, she would greet the client by saying, "Hey, Boobie!" Thus, since I've been married to her son, I've affectionately called her "Mother Boobie Dear."

I am blessed beyond words to have Mother Boobie Dear in my life! When most women talk about their mother-in-law, it is with disdain and accompanied by eye rolls that send a clear message that their husbands' moms are not their most favorite people in the world. However, my relationship with Mother Boobie Dear is different; we are *genuinely* like best friends. People typically find this difficult to believe, but it's true! We are so close that it gets on my husband's nerves. We can easily talk on the phone for an hour and a half about anything and everything, because she is so cool – so relatable and understanding. In fact, there are some things that I do not feel comfortable talking about to anyone else except my Mother Boobie Dear, because with her, no topic is off limits. I think she really understands me. My mother-in-law is also my favorite house guest; I even get off work early when she's in town to hang out with her, shopping, eating, talking and just enjoying one another's company.

The day that I was first diagnosed with cancer, Mother Boobie Dear was one of the first people that I called with the news. As soon as she picked up the phone, I began crying and complaining about how it was so unfair for me to have cancer. However, she didn't give me her pity.

"First of all," she said, "we're gonna stop crying and we're gonna fight this!"

"Did you hear what I just said? I said I have cancer. CANCER! Can you just let me have today to be sad and feel sorry for myself?" I asked.

"Unh unh. Nope! We're gonna fight this," she said.

Much later, she told me that at that moment, she knew that she had to be tough for me. However, as soon as she hung up the phone, she completely lost it. My Mother Boobie Dear has a tough exterior, but she is one of the sweetest and most loving people you'll ever meet.

I remember the year that we went to a women's church conference, *Woman Thou Art Loosed*, together. We went to all of the workshops and services, and we were having an amazing time at the conference. One night, we were just sitting around in the sanctuary following a powerful worship service; it was one of those services that caused people to want to linger in God's presence afterwards, crying, praying at the altar, and sharing with one another. Mother Boobie Dear and I were sitting on the steps of the stage. All of a sudden, she just grabbed me and hugged me tightly. She said, "Little girl, I love you just like I gave birth to you myself!" I love her so much! I wish every wife could have a relationship with their mother-in-law like I have with mine. I wouldn't want to be on this journey without her!

I also wouldn't want to be on this journey without Ms. Pat. Our friendship started with her serving as my assistant at our church in Richmond, I was initially hesitant about having an assistant; however, after hearing about the misfortunes of another colleague, my husband insisted that I have an assistant to work with me at our church and for all ministry related events. As a matter of fact, my husband met Ms. Pat at her new member's class. He came home ecstatic and informed me that he found someone who I'd really like to have as an assistant. I met Ms. Pat and we just clicked!

She is like a mother, sister, friend, and assistant all-in-one! We laugh all the time – at ourselves! She travels everywhere with me. No one says "Oh my God" or "Oh my word" like she does. She taught me the importance of getting rest. After all, she is a sleep expert. Lastly, once my sister could no longer miss work to attend my chemo sessions, Ms. Pat picked up where she left off. Make sure that you have someone whom you can trust and laugh with on your journey!

Finally, in addition to my family, my friends are must-have travel companions on this journey. I have different groups of friends. I have one group of friends that I get together with, my favorite, and we are so close that we consider ourselves to be a little club. We each have titles and everything. I'm the CEO, because I'm the one in charge. I lead our "top secret" club business when we get together, usually about once a month. We'll go to a restaurant, go through our "organizational business," and laugh for hours – literally. It's so much fun! Even when I'm not feeling well, I'll put on a game face while I'm getting dressed so my husband won't recommend that I stay home and miss one of our famously fun "meetings." In fact, although I might leave the house not feeling my best, after I spend hours laughing with these ladies, I often come back feeling so much better. The Bible says that laughter, or a cheerful heart, is good medicine, and I'm a witness to the truth of this! On those rare days that I get home after our "meeting" and realize that I don't feel great at all, I never regret going. It's always worth it! I simply take my pain meds and then sit back, reflecting on the amazing friends I'm blessed to have.

Another group of friends that I love dearly is my group of friends from college. We've known each other for a long time: we attended middle school, high school, and college together. In college, we lived together as suite mates; two of us in one bedroom, and the other two in a bedroom, with the two bedrooms separated by one bathroom, which we shared. Although we all kind of went our own ways and built our own lives after college, we remain close to this day. In fact, we took a girls trip to Las Vegas in 2017, and it was a blast. There we were, all together again in one hotel room with everyone talking a mile a minute followed by loud outbursts of laughter! During the day, we would go on adventures like visiting the Grand Canyon, shopping, eating at different restaurants, and seeing the sights. At the end of the day, we would sit around in our pj's all night talking, catching everyone up on our lives, crying, playing spades, ordering room service, eating, and just enjoying one another. It was such an unforgettable time. We recently had another fun reunion for my 45th birthday celebration. They all traveled to Richmond to spend a cold snowy weekend with me and it was simply fantastic.

My husband and I also have one couple who we consider to be our best friends and favorite traveling companions, Theresa and Darrick. They are the type of ride or die friends that we all need. They are also extremely resourceful. We all work hard and play hard. On a trip to California, I was surprised to see them appear at our hotel. The even bigger surprise was that Theresa had secured four tickets for one of my favorite game shows, "Let's Make a Deal!" I *love* game shows!

We drove to a store to create some costumes. We went to the taping and to my surprise, my husband and I were selected as contestants! We walked away with a bedroom set and $300. However, the experience and time with our friends can't be replaced. God has blessed me with such funny, amazing friends, and I'm so grateful to have each and every one of them as a traveling companion with me on this journey!

Item 8: "Grace Passes" for the Not-So-Well Behaved

Have you ever had the misfortune of sitting on a plane next to a person that invaded your space, talked too much, or was obnoxious or unpleasant in some way? I'm sure that you did what we do when we encounter such people: you gave them grace. You just endured the flight, knowing it would be over soon. You didn't let them ruin your trip. You simply chalked it up to, "That's the way people are." It wasn't that you condoned their behavior. It's just that you realized that you had two options: "go off" on them or just walk away. You're a classy person, so you just shook your head, breathed a heavy sigh, walked away, and kept things moving along on your journey. You gave them a pass – a grace pass.

Here's a heads-up: you're going to need a lot of grace passes along your journey through adversity. People are going to say the wrong thing, do the wrong thing, be mean and obnoxious to you for no reason, fail to give you the level of understanding you deserve in light of your current situation, and display a general lack of sensitivity to what you're going through at the time. In such situations, you have to simply give people grace. Forgive them and move on, not allowing them to ruffle your feathers. What else are you going to do? I can guarantee that any alternative to giving them a grace pass would violate one of the aspects of a sparkling through adversity mentality! Remember: people are watching you sparkle, so all eyes are on you, especially when they see someone trying your patience and kindness. If you're going to sparkle on this journey, you're going to have to extend a lot of grace to people who you feel might not even deserve it. Therefore, pack *a lot* of grace passes for your journey.

I could tell you story after story of how I've had to give grace passes to people along my own journey. For example, there's one story that I think about often where I encountered the meanest, nastiest person ever in my career. After I was diagnosed with cancer, I went to the central administration office for the school district where I worked. I explained that I had been diagnosed with stage 4 cancer and would immediately begin chemotherapy. My immune system would be weakened, and it was not a good idea for me to be working in the classroom around the many germs that the students had. I asked if they could find a different position for me, hoping they would transfer me to an administrative position. There were better positions with better pay that were open; I'd already checked. They would have been a promotion from my current title, and I was completely qualified for them.

The lady that I was speaking to gave me a different position – she transferred me to a specialty school for students referred for severe behavioral challenges. Specialty schools for students referred for severe behavior can be challenging. This is the type of school filled with troubled students... the kind where a student could lose his temper and throw a desk or a chair across the room at me at any moment. I simply couldn't understand this. I had a Ph.D.! I had the training. I had over 20 years of experience. I had a special education certificate. At the time, I was working on my administration certificate. She could have easily put someone of my caliber in a safer, professional administrative position in the central office. Instead, she thought it was a good idea to put me, a cancer patient with a doctorate, in a dangerous and challenging environment. What's worse, when I applied for FMLA (Family Medical Leave Act) to take leave from my job as I began my first rounds of chemo, her question to me was, "Leave? Well you're not going to have cancer forever, are you?"

I could not believe my ears. Before then, I never would have thought that a person could be so mean and heartless towards me. However, I had to give her a grace pass. I let it go. I kept silent and trusted God to work things out for me.

As it turned out, what this mean, nasty woman in the central office meant for evil, God meant for good. He ended up turning things around and used this demotion as a platform for promotion in the midst of my journey! When I got assigned to the specialty school, I went there and gave it all I had. I soon found out that the principal of the school, who oversaw three different schools, needed an assistant principal. He'd been interviewing people over and over again for the position, but no one was the right fit for the position. Finally, the position was closed and taken off the table. When I heard about it, I said, "Okay, God. I'm going to take the initiative and go for this position." After talking to the principal, applying, interviewing and beating another candidate out for the job, I got the call from Human Resources: I got the position! I couldn't believe it. I went to the bathroom and just cried. It was a better position with better pay, and it took me out of the danger of the classroom. Today, I love my job, my staff, and everything that I do. I can't wait to get up and go to work every day. In fact, even when I'm not feeling well, I never like to take off; I just get up and go to this place that I love. See how God turned that around? I gave the lady a grace pass, and He took it from there.

Another instance when I had to offer a grace pass to someone was at church. One Sunday, I wasn't feeling my best, but I came to church anyway, because as I mentioned before, I love church. I *need* church. As I sat there trying to look my best and hoping that I didn't look as terribly sickly as I felt, my pastor husband asked everyone in the church to keep me in their prayers. He explained that I wasn't feeling well and that he'd asked me to stay home, but I'd come to church anyway because I loved being there and interacting with the people. He also gave clear instructions that, if people were going to hug me, they should give me very soft hugs in order to not hurt me.

I never wanted to be the kind of "untouchable" first lady that didn't interact with people, so even though I wasn't feeling well, I hung around church for a few minutes after the morning service had ended. It was during this time that a lady came up to me and said, "Oooh! You just look *tired* today!" I was so taken aback. I was stunned. I wouldn't expect for anyone to ever say something so insensitive to me considering that I have cancer. I feel that if you are going to say something to someone who's going through such a difficult time, your words should be positive. You should try to make them feel better. Any words that aren't positive or affirming simply shouldn't be said! I simply couldn't understand the purpose behind her words. Did she really think her words were going to uplift me or help me feel better? Or worse, was she deliberately trying to make me feel worse than I already did… and why? Initially, the lady's words kind of hurt my feelings. Then, the more I thought about it, they made me mad. However, I didn't say anything to her. I didn't confront or rebuke her. I gave her a grace pass. I let it go and walked away, even though it was probably the worst Sunday I'd ever had. I felt really, really bad, both physically and emotionally.

I ended up going into the back office of the church and sharing what happened with my husband. I told him I felt some kind of way about it. My husband being the protective husband that he is made sure that he addressed it the next time he took the pulpit. He shared that someone had gone to me and told me that I looked tired. Then, he encouraged the people to be mindful of what they said to one another, especially when they know that someone is going through something. He explained that if words weren't positive and uplifting, they shouldn't be spoken at all. Despite how terrible the lady made me feel, I didn't try to make her feel bad at all. That was another grace pass.

I could go on and on about the different interactions that I've had with people on my journey that often require a grace pass. They happen more than you might think! Here are some of the most common:

* People find out that I have cancer, and they reply with, "Oh, really? I have a family member who died of cancer." Then, they go on to tell me the stories about all the people they know who died from cancer. Just an FYI, that's the wrong thing to say to someone with cancer. If it's not a story about someone surviving, thriving and happy in life, I don't want to hear it! I don't want to hear any bad news. I don't even go online to Google things about breast cancer or any of my symptoms or side effects, because they bring me anxiety. There are some details that I just don't want to know about what others have experienced and what I might eventually experience. Let me just find out on my own. In any case, I give them a grace pass.

* People give me what I call "cancer gifts." I've been given scarves with the pink cancer awareness ribbon and even a cancer Bible. I personally don't feel like cancer is who I am; it's just something I'm dealing with in this current season of my life. Gifts like these make me say, "So my whole life is just gonna be about cancer? That's all you see when you look at me? Why not just get me a gift card? I do still wear shoes and clothes, you know?" Even though these things frustrate me and make me want to withdraw and not be around people at all, I know that they had good intentions. I give them a grace pass.

* People say, "You know, that chemotherapy is really bad for your body! It does a lot of damage to your insides and tears you up. Why don't you try a natural homeopathic remedy instead?" Then, they go on to give me their own prescriptions, supplements, health foods, and natural remedies that are supposed to cure my cancer. Some people also send me stuff like teas, oils, etc. Such audacity! Do they really think I'm going to just stop listening to my doctor and start listening to them? If it's not recommended by my oncologist or one of my medical doctor friends whom I trust, I'm not using it! What my doctor is doing for me is working just fine. Again, I know that they're just trying to be helpful. I even appreciate that they were thinking about me enough to pick something up for me that they think will help me (even though there's no way I'm going to use it). I give them a grace pass.

People often lack discretion, wisdom, good sense, or whatever it is that a person lacks when they say things that come out wrong when someone is going through a difficult journey. It doesn't have to be cancer. People are known to say the wrong thing when a person is dealing with the loss of a loved one, a divorce, a serious domestic matter, a huge financial transition, another illness or disease... you name it. Of course, they don't mean to hurt or offend; I think a lot of times, they just don't know any better. Their motives are pure… or at the very least not thought through very well at all. Therefore, when people say and do the wrong thing, give them a grace pass.

You want to know the best thing you can say to someone who's going through a difficult journey? Just say the following: "I'm thinking about you, and I'm praying that everything works out for you." That's it. Keep it simple. Stay away from long stories, because the more you talk, the more you're likely to stray away from discretion, say the wrong thing and need a grace pass of your own.

Item 9: A Journal

There's nothing like having adventures along your travels, and then at the end of the day, having some time to yourself when you can pull out your journal and quietly reflect on all of the things that happened that day. Not only does journaling allow you to recount all of the details of the events of the day, both good and bad, but it allows you the opportunity to process what happened. Journaling helps you to work through how you feel, what you think, your position on things, and helps you to pour all of your ideas out onto paper. Then, at the end of your travels, when you get back home, your journal serves as a permanent written record that helps you to remember not only what happened, but what you thought and felt about what happened. They say that a picture is worth a thousand words, but pictures are still limited in what they can say; there are some things that you should actually put into words yourself. The best way to do this is by setting aside a dedicated time to put your reflections down in a journal.

One thing that I've learned by going through a journey of adversity is that there are things that I can talk to people about, and then there are things that it is best that I not mention to anyone. However, it is also unhealthy to keep the things that you can't mention to others pent up on the inside; this only creates more stress and tension in the body. These thoughts and feelings *need* to be expressed – *purged*! A journal is the perfect place to pour these things out freely and for your eyes only (unless you opt to share).

As you go through your own journey of adversity, I recommend keeping either a written or an electronic journal. I've been keeping a journal since I began my chemo treatments. After all, I had nothing but time as I sat in the chair receiving my treatment, so I thought I would make productive use of it. During these times, I would write in my journal about everything from my fears to my hopes and dreams. I would record my frustrations as well as my triumphs and testimonies. My journal has remained my private, safe space, a place where I can write anything I want without fear of judgment or critique. I know that in the end, when I get to the other side of my journey, I will have an intimate written record of all that God has delivered me through for His glory. What I'm going through and learning on my journey are things that I never want to forget!

Item 10: Meds

There's nothing like investing your money, time and energy into planning a journey, only to get there and not feel well enough to enjoy it. Therefore, it's necessary to put meds, or medications, on your packing list. Many of the other things in your baggage are meant to help you *look* your best. Meds, however, are brought along on the journey to help you *feel* your best, which is important.

My particular journey is health related, so for me, it's necessary to pack meds, both literally and figuratively. I have to literally pack my actual meds because my doctor has prescribed them for me to take on a daily basis in order to maintain my health and wellness – to feel better. Your journey through adversity may not be health related; you might need things other than prescription or over-the-counter meds to maintain your health and wellness and feel better. In this case, you need to pack your meds in a figurative sense.

Anything that makes you feel better amidst the adversity that you are experiencing on your journey, especially when you begin feeling your worst, can be considered a "med." Only you know what your meds are – what you turn to in order to feel good when the circumstances of your adversity are making you feel bad. For example, one of the meds that I take to help myself feel better is music, particularly music from my favorites, the legendary Clark Sisters. Any time I listen to the Clark Sisters, it's like medicine for my soul, so I keep this med close by for when I need a dose of it. I love to listen to the Clark Sisters when I'm riding in my car and when I'm at home by myself, turning up the volume to give myself the biggest dose possible! Music drowns out everything going on around me, especially all of the bad feelings and negativity, making it a must-have med on the packing list for my journey.

Another one of the meds that I can't do without on my journey through adversity is laughter. The Bible says that "a cheerful heart is good medicine" (Proverbs 17:22), and I'm a witness to this; laughter is good medicine for the soul. Laughter has helped me to get through some of the roughest patches on my journey, making me feel better even when my actual medications could not. There's a physiological reason for this. Researchers have found that laughter leads to a reduction in stress hormones in the body. Laughter also causes the brain to release endorphins, which can literally relieve some of our physical pain. Medical scientists have also found that laughter enhances the disease-fighting cells (T-cells) in the body and boosts the count of the cells that produce antibodies, which results in a stronger immune system. God has fearfully and wonderfully created our bodies to respond to the healing properties of laughter, so why not pack it as a med on the journey?

Recently, I had a really rough day at chemo. Another guy who was receiving a treatment nearby was also struggling and having a really rough time. It was a really tense moment for the both of us, and I was almost in tears. In the midst of our struggle, I looked over at him and caught his eye. I said, "You know what time it is!"... and then we just began laughing. We weren't laughing at anything in particular; having an actual, identifiable reason to laugh is not a prerequisite for laughing. We laughed and laughed, and it eased the tension of the moment, making us both feel a little better. We laugh at ourselves a lot, sometimes for a funny reason, and sometimes for no reason at all. Thank God for the med of laughter!

7

Being confident of this very thing, that he which hath begun a good work in you will perform it until the day of Jesus Christ – Phillipians 1:6

THE MUSIC IN MY HEART: INSPIRING THE WORLD WITH SONGS OF FAITH & MY SPARKLE

For me to be standing on stages and singing for the Lord was inevitable. I was destined to be in the church and involved in music. I say this for two reasons. First, I come from a church family; everyone in my family is either a preacher, a preacher's wife, or is in music ministry in the church. My parents are preachers, my grandparents were preachers, my uncles are all pastors, and my aunts are all married to preachers. Everyone who doesn't preach either sings or plays a musical instrument. With such a strong spiritual legacy behind me, it's no wonder that I'm doing what I do today.

The second reason that I think I was destined to be in the church and involved in music is because of something that happened to me when I was a young girl. My mother raised me, my younger brother (who is a professional percussionist) and my younger sister (who is an organist and a singer) in Baltimore in a Christian home. My mother got married to a strict Pentecostal preacher when I was eight years old. One day, my dad called me up and said, "This morning, we're going to have a song by Taleshia!" That was news to me! Even though he'd said my name, I was looking around like, "Taleshia, who?" I just sat there. What was he asking me to sing for? I wasn't a singer! What was he thinking?

I tried to wait him out, sitting in my seat and refusing to go up to sing, but my dad didn't give in at all; he demanded that I obey him and sing a song. It took a while for me to realize that he was really going to make me sing, and when I realized it, I began to cry. The tears didn't work. Upset, I reluctantly walked to the front of the small, 10-member church and stood by the organ, which my mother was playing. "All God's Children" was the first song I ever sang in the church. I've been singing for His glory ever since.

Because my family had such deep roots in the church, growing up, I was determined that I was never going to marry a preacher. I wanted to marry someone who went to church, but I didn't want him to be the preacher. Well, you know how that went, right? The love of my life, whom I met in high school, received his call while we were dating, and he is now a pastor. Our relationship has always been centered on ministry; he's always been the preacher, and I've always been his first lady – his *singing* first lady! Little did I know that the day my dad called me up to sing in front of our little church for the very first time, God was preparing me for the life in ministry that was nowhere in my plans. He was also preparing me by using me in every other role possible in the church as a young girl; I served as an usher, in the choir, collected the money... you name it. By the time I began walking by my pastor-husband's side as his helpmate in ministry, I knew church and music ministry inside-out, and I'd developed the confidence I needed to fulfill my role with excellence.

I've always ministered in song at my own church, and sometimes, I would get invited to other local churches to sing. However, nothing could have prepared me for the opportunities that I would have to minister in song for the Lord after I wrote my first book, sharing my testimony about the *Divine Detour* that God is taking me on several years ago. There were people who had heard my story, and they were inspired by it. In addition to having me come share my testimony and do book signings, they asked me to minister in song. Music is a part of who I am, so I gladly agreed to do so. Initially, as I began touring around to different places for this purpose, I thought I would be intimidated by all of the new faces and big crowds. However, I believe that all of the years I'd spent singing for the Lord, including on my church's praise team, prepared me for it. I was completely at ease.

Remember the amazing friends that I told you about? The ones that I feel so privileged to have as traveling companions on my journey? They ensure that I don't travel alone when I go out to minister at other churches. I have about five of them to choose from to help me when I travel, and if I'm singing locally, they all still come out and support me wherever I'm singing. Their presence also helps to put me at ease. It's always good to have familiar faces in the crowd that you know are there for you and praying for you. Their presence helps me to sparkle just a little brighter.

Typically, when it's time for me to minister, I begin with briefly sharing my testimony so that people can see my sparkle. What I don't want is for the people in the crowd to think that I'm a person with cancer who is struggling, scared and sad about my situation. I don't want them to feel sorry for me at all. Instead, my testimony is all about the sparkle. I want them to see someone who is polished, pulled together, strong, beautiful, sparkling instead of hiding, full of faith, and walking in victory. I'm there to inspire them; I'm not there for them to inspire me! I usually begin my "sparkle testimony" with something like this:

It's such a blessing for me to be here with you today. As you can see, I may have lost my hair, but I haven't lost my faith! I realize that I'm bald, but that doesn't take away from my trust in God. I still believe that He's able. I don't know when or how, but I know He's going to heal me! When someone dies, a lot of people will say, "They fought a good battle, but God has truly healed them, because they're in heaven now and don't have to experience any pain." Well, my prayer is that God will heal me, but I want to be alive to share my testimony with even more people. I'm now cancer free. Well, I want to be alive to say that to people so that they'll know that my God is awesome! I don't feel any shame in saying this. I know that our prayer should be, "Whatever Your will is, Lord!" I pray that His will is that I'm alive to share my story of healing. I'm confident that He can get me through this, and I know that He can do the same for you!

Then, I launch into a song that God has laid on my heart to minister. I have two favorite songs that I love to minister when I travel to and share my testimony. The first is "Yesterday" by Mary Mary. I love singing this song because there have been times when I have literally cried myself to sleep asking God, "Why? Why does this have to be the tool that You use to make me fulfill my purpose of traveling, singing, ministering to and inspiring other people? Why would you use the one disease that I was most afraid of getting?" I just cried and cried. I can't even tell you how many times I cried, especially that first year. I cried so much that it was hard to sleep. That's why this song means so much to me. The lyrics say, "I decided that I cried my last tear yesterday," and talk trusting God and about how there's nothing too hard for God, because He's greater than anything we face. These words deeply resonate with me because they capture how I feel about my journey so well. Yes, I might have another crying moment; after all, I'm only human. However, I always get up and minister the song with all my heart, because even though I might cry a tear or two when I'm not feeling so confident and strong, I've come a long way from where I began.

My other favorite song to minister is "Trust Me" by Richard Smallwood. The reason that I love this song is because it sums up my testimony. In fact, my love for the song continues to grow day by day; I love it more today than yesterday. The lyrics are written as if God is saying, He'll be with me, never leave me, and fight my battle if I trust in Him. They talk about how God says that He has all power to deliver if I just trust in Him. I can truly say that through all of the bad days, chemo treatments, tests, CT scans, echocardiograms, intense pain, surgery, shots, blood draws, radiation, hair loss, and other things I've had to endure over the past several years, I've maintained my trust the Lord. I've asked "Why?" but I've never wavered in my faith by failing to believe that He can heal me. I know that He's with me, and He has the power to deliver me out of what I'm going through, but I've got to trust Him – and I do. I don't know how He's going to get me out of this, but I truly believe at some point, I'm going to go to my doctor for my CT scan, and he's going to say, "Taleshia, we can't find anything." That is why I sing this song. I trust God.

I don't just sing to sing. I'm not a performer; I'm a minister. I sing to inspire others to believe that God is with them and to give them hope that He can do anything in their lives, no matter how difficult the situation. Every time I minister, I do so with this mission in mind. From the way I present myself, to the testimony I share, to the song that I sing, it's all about moving people – inspiring them to believe God while they are going through adversity. As a result, I'm blessed to say that there are so many people in my life that have been encouraged to continue in their faith and believe God.

I see now, more than ever before, that God has allowed me to go on my own journey in order to learn how to inspire people – to show them how to sparkle through their own adversity. There are so many examples of this, but I do have a couple of favorites. For example, there's my friend Ms. Pat who's also my assistant (you met her in chapter 6). We went out on a Friday night, and she was telling me about her only son. She mentioned how she was worried about the group of guys he had been hanging around with and how much she only wanted the best for him. That very next day, early in the morning, she called me and said her son had been shot. Of course, my husband and I rushed to get ready and get to the hospital. While we were on our way, she called and said he was gone – just like that. It was a really difficult situation.

For a long time, Pat was in a sad, very depressed place. This was her only child. After that, we would be talking about something funny, and we would laugh together. Then, she would catch herself, saying that she felt that it was wrong for her to be happy and have a good time when her son was gone. She drew back into her depressed state. I challenged her to sparkle rather than falling back into depression. I asked, "Don't you think he'd want you to be happy and enjoy life? Did you not give him everything and do your best for him? Didn't you put him in all of the best schools? Weren't you a great mother?" She would say "Yes" to all of these. I helped her to acknowledge that she'd done her absolute best with her son; the decisions that he made were all his own.

I talked to Pat constantly, encouraging her to think about all of the good memories that she'd made with her son while he was alive, thanking God for every moment that she was blessed to have him. Then, I helped her to see why and how she should celebrate and maximize her life each and every day, despite her grief. Over time, she gradually began getting back to life, sparkling through her grief instead of allowing it to overtake her life. She began taking walks through the park, traveling, and laughing without feeling guilty about it. She fixed up her son's old car, because it made her feel like she was doing something for him – something in his honor. Despite her grief and the empty place in her heart caused by losing her only child, she's still able to feel joyful and enjoy life without him. Now, Pat is paying it forward; she's helping other people who are going through traumas and tragedies to learn how to sparkle through their own devastating situations.

The reason that I love to use Pat as an example is because what I taught her about sparkling through her journey and enjoying life despite the pain she feels, she is turning around and sharing with others. I have no doubt that the people she helps will help others, who will help others, and so on. The number of people who will be helped by Pat and the lives she touches is unlimited!

Just as I was able to inspire Pat, it's my desire to add you to the list of those whom I have inspired and that you, in turn, inspire others. Working together, we can touch thousands of lives, helping them to sparkle and shine through the hardest seasons of their lives. Sparkling through adversity isn't easy; you haven't once heard me make such a claim. Getting yourself together physically, emotionally, mentally, and otherwise so that others can look at your life and be inspired by you is challenging! However, sparkling through adversity and going through your situation with joy, faith, style and grace is something that is *possible* for everyone to do – including you – regardless of the situation. If you're willing to take the initiative and responsibility to put in some work in order to sparkle instead of just sitting around and pray about your situation, you'll see a drastic difference in how you go through the toughest journey of your life. That's my guarantee, and I have God to back me up on it!

May the Lord be with you as you sparkle through your journey, and may all of those who have the privilege of witnessing your shine be inspired to sparkle themselves!

ABOUT THE AUTHOR

Dr. Taleshia Lenshell Chandler serves as the first lady of the Cedar Street Baptist Church in Richmond, VA where her husband is the senior pastor.

A popular invited guest psalmist, Dr. Chandler has ministered around the country at churches, conferences and conventions, sharing her powerful music ministry gift for decades. She ministers with a heavy anointing; people report being ushered into the presence of God and experiencing hope, healing and breakthroughs like never before under the sound of her voice.

Dr. Chandler is the author of two books: *A Divine Detour: From Doctorate to Diagnosis to Destiny*, which chronicles her journey and offers hope for others who have experienced life-changing circumstances and *Sparking through Adversity: Traveling through Life's Toughest Journeys with Style, Grace & Shine!*, in which she shares practical lessons on how to not look like what you're going through while enduring some of life's most difficult challenges.

A passionate educator, Dr. Chandler has worked in the public school system for more than 20 years and is an adjunct psychology instructor for the University of Phoenix. She resides in Glen Allen, VA with her high school sweetheart and husband of 22 years, Dr. Anthony M. Chandler, Sr. They are the proud parents of Anthony Michael, Alysha Michelle, and Andrew Maxwell.

50067472R00080

Made in the USA
Middletown, DE
22 June 2019